SIAN HILL

Driven For Success

Activate Your Winning Formula

First published by Formerly titled – Activate Your RAS – The Art & Science of Creating Your Reality from the Inside Out 2025

Second edition

ISBN (paperback): 978-1-7391772-8-7
ISBN (hardcover): 978-1-7391772-9-4

This book was professionally typeset on Reedsy.
Find out more at reedsy.com

Contents

Acknowledgments

Writing this book has been a journey that has stretched and challenged me in countless ways. It would not have been possible without the unwavering support of my wonderful Mum and Dad.

To my mum – thank you for being my sounding board, my first proofreader, my researcher and, in truth, an unpaid team member who wore many hats. You gave so freely of your time and energy, taking on whatever I asked of you without hesitation and for that I am endlessly grateful.

To my dad – despite your own health struggles, you always found ways to support me. You lightened my load by taking on daily tasks, giving me the space to focus on writing and constantly offering your help. Both of you have been a tower of strength, encouraging me, cheering me on and believing in me every step of the way.

To my partner, Dan – thank you for always encouraging me to follow my dreams, even when it meant so many evenings spent tucked away writing. Your unwavering belief in me has never faltered. You remind me that I can achieve anything I set my mind to and in the midst of challenges, you've brought laughter and lightness, helping me keep perspective along the way.

To my dear friend Jeanette – my cheerleader, confidante and constant source of encouragement. You insisted that the world needed to hear my message and on the days I doubted myself, you offered to be the one who listened, reminding me that my words mattered. Your faith in me has been a gift I will always treasure.

Finally, I want to acknowledge and thank my teachers and leaders in the field of personal transformation. Many of you I have never met, yet your teachings have had a profound impact on my life. The wisdom you have shared has shaped not only this book but also the person I have become.

Introduction

The best way to win the game is to know the rules no one else sees.

It was just another Tuesday afternoon. There was nothing out of the ordinary happening, except for the red car. It seemed to be following me. The funny thing was, I'd never noticed it before, yet now it was everywhere. I found myself wondering whether it had always been there.

I'd only thought about the red car for the first time the day before and suddenly it was on every street corner, every driveway, even the supermarket car park. What on earth was going on?

Let me backtrack.

A week earlier, I was introduced to a new way of thinking – a concept that felt both impossibly simple and profoundly true – we, as human beings, possess an internal mechanism that can be leveraged to create our reality. The idea was that our thoughts influence our reality – not in a mystical way, but because what we focus on shapes our decisions, behaviours and the opportunities we notice. In that sense, our thoughts become things: imagining something as true in your mind doesn't magically create it, but it does influence how you show up and what you move towards. It wasn't about wishing on a star; it was about understanding how the mind works, reprogramming unhelpful patterns and using it deliberately to support our ambitions.

This was a radical idea for someone who had always believed that success was a matter of pure hard work and luck. I was intrigued and, frankly, desperate to find any advantage. I had a backlog of goals I wanted to achieve, so I had some catching up to do! I decided to test the concept using that shiny red car I'd been fantasising about.

My interpretation at the time was that all I needed to do was picture the life I desired and it would arrive. Whether it was a promotion, business opportunities, or something as small as a new dress, all that was required was to visualise it. So, I let my imagination wander as I pictured myself behind the wheel, my hands on the leather, the sun on my face, singing along to my favourite songs with the windows down.

It was only a few days later that the strange thing happened. The car, which I had previously believed was a rare, unique model, began showing up everywhere.

I felt a surge of excitement, but also a wave of confusion. I was doing the mental work and the "evidence" was showing up, but what was I supposed to do with it? Was it a sign?

My understanding, from the little I had read, was that if I

could see it in my mind, it would arrive on my driveway, but I couldn't afford a car payment, let alone the insurance. I wondered if I should take a loan and just "trust the process." After all, I was seeing the car everywhere. This was proof I was on track, right?

What I really wanted to know was... WHAT WAS THE SHINY RED CAR TELLING ME?

Of course, this experience isn't just limited to cars. It's relevant to every desire, every goal, every dream you have and your ability to take it from idea and bring it into the tangible world we live in.

When I first discovered that I had the power to use my mind to change how I experienced the world and my interactions with it, I took everything as a sign. I would play a song I loved for the first time in years and it then seemed to be playing everywhere I went – in shops, bars, on the radio – and it wasn't even popular. I'd hunt for hidden meanings in the lyrics, convinced they were a personal message just for me.

After really enjoying a particular brand of peanut butter at a friend's house and wanting some for myself, there it was on the shelf in every supermarket and every corner shop I entered. It appeared on adverts, billboards, leaflets, but I could've sworn it hadn't existed before the first day I put it on my toast.

My mind was made up... I wanted a cat and just like that, the world seemed to fill with them. Identical lookalikes lived across the street, down the road and even appeared on cat food bags.. I had to ask myself: Had they always been there? If so, how had I missed them?

More importantly, how could I use this information to my advantage?

My initial introduction to the understanding that our inner world, our thoughts and feelings, create our outer experience came through a book about the universal law known as the Law of Attraction.

The Law of Attraction states that like attracts like; thoughts become things and you can manifest anything you want. 'Manifest' means to bring something into existence. The basic concept is that we are energy and all energy has a frequency to it that vibrates at a specific rate. Just like magnets, when frequencies are a vibrational match, they attract each other. When our thoughts are a match to the things we desire, they become our reality and so you get what you think about. It made sense. I'd thought about all of those things – the car, the song, the peanut butter, the cat – and so there they were, showing up everywhere, although not necessarily on my driveway!

Back to my earlier question, what did those things showing up actually mean and what was I supposed to do with that information?

After extensive reading, I came to a simple, yet ultimately flawed, conclusion. I was on the right path to creating the things I wanted. Seeing these items constantly was proof I was "vibrationally aligned" – the universe was giving me the green light. It was a sign! And my interpretation of this sign was an invitation to act.

This meant if I wanted to create a new life, I had to behave as if I already had it. The message I internalised was, "If you see it, it's yours and trust. Act as if it's a done deal." So, I did. I took out a loan, convinced that the money for the red car and my mountain of bills would simply appear. I told myself it was about stepping outside my comfort zone, but in reality, it didn't turn out to be quite that simple and I very quickly discovered there was a difference between stepping outside of what felt comfortable, trusting that everything would work out and putting myself in a position that was doomed to fail from the start.

I barely had the money to eat, let alone treat myself to the car I had been eyeing up that was way out of my price range. I continued to visualise success – the money rolling into my bank account every day, the shiny red car on my driveway, a handsome stranger arriving on a white horse to "rescue" me, a dream job being offered out of the blue.

It turned out that just trusting money would appear, whilst simultaneously losing sleep over my ever-growing list of bills, didn't actually work in the way I'd hoped! But I was stubborn and wanted to prove I could do it, that visualising the life I wanted would bring it into my experience and so I persevered. It took me a while to recognise there was more than just imagination required to pay for the material things I wanted. Whilst I believed anything was possible, that logic didn't necessarily apply to me and I managed to get myself into debt at an impressive rate. The lack of belief and results very quickly became a never-ending cycle of negativity that kept feeding itself. A cycle that I couldn't seem to find a way out of.

I tried visualising and it didn't work, which proved that I was a failure...

I believed I was a failure, so I behaved like a failure... Behaving like a failure led to the results of failing...

I proved myself right... Aha! I thought I was a failure and I was right!

Round and round the cycle went with what felt like no exit point in sight. The more I thought about it, the more evidence I gathered that it was true, making the belief stronger every time. What this agonising loop ultimately proved to me was a powerful truth: our thoughts really do become things.

I'm sure you've had one, or more likely many, of your own self-fulfilling prophecy cycles that you can't seem to break.

After many months of taking little action and hoping my lottery ticket would be the answer (it wasn't), I was frustrated and ready to take control. But my desires were still far bigger than my belief in my ability to achieve them. The action I took was a direct reflection of that self-doubt... very little. There was an obvious mismatch between what I wanted and what I thought was even probable, let alone likely.

So, I went back to the original question... what was the shiny red car, or any other object of my desire, really trying to tell me? I was finally ready for an answer that wasn't a platitude or a wish, but a function of my own mind. And that's when I found the missing piece of the puzzle: your RAS.

Meet Your RAS

Let me introduce you... (I'll keep the science brief for now!)

Your RAS, short for reticular activating system, is a tiny but powerful part of the brain. It sits at the top of the spinal column, stretching upward just a couple of inches, about as wide as a pencil. Inside that little area is a dense bundle of nerves.

All of your senses - everything you see, hear, feel and taste – are wired to the neurons in that bundle; everything that is, except for your sense of smell, which takes a direct shortcut to the emotional centre of your brain. All day, every second, your senses are bombarded with far more information than you could ever consciously process.

That's where your RAS comes in. Think of it like a radar system. It's constantly scanning, filtering through the flood of sensory data, based on what matters and what doesn't. What it flags as important, it activates and sends a signal to your conscious mind, bringing that very thing to your attention. The rest fades into the background, outside of your awareness.

Your RAS is essentially the gatekeeper of your conscious mind!

That red car was mentally tagged as important, so my RAS let the information through to my conscious mind and instantly alerted me to its presence.

This is why your RAS plays such a crucial role in creating results and why it's worth getting to know. Every day, opportunities and potential pathways to your success are metaphorically knocking at your door. Still, if your RAS isn't primed to recognise them, they'll pass you by unnoticed and you won't know they even exist.

So, the real question becomes, how does your RAS know when to activate? When it does, what can you do with that information? And perhaps most importantly, how do you change its signal if your activation is not aligned with your goals?

This book is going to explain exactly that!

To set the tone for what we'll cover, it's important to first mention that the reality you know isn't actually reality at all. It's only your perception of it which, ironically, is therefore your reality. Now, saying this is all very well and good, but if you're anything like me, you're probably wondering what it really means and, more importantly, what you can do about it.

There's an old saying, dating back centuries, from the Greek god Hermes Trismegistus:

"As within, so without."

This statement is very true. You really do create your experience from the inside out, which means you do indeed have the ability to purposefully achieve your goals. Powerful stuff, right? Of course, only when you know how to change your internal world, that is!

There is another saying:

"Knowledge is power."

Also true. Well, it's half the story anyway. Knowledge does indeed have the potential to be powerful, but it only goes so far. Knowing something isn't the same as doing it and the real power lies in the application of the knowledge.

Let's face it, everyone knows that eating well and regular exercise are a big part of what makes you physically healthy, but knowing this doesn't change anything unless you use that knowledge to take action. Yet, without that knowledge, where would you begin?

Whether you're competing in sport, building an empire, or working on a personal goal to get to a specific waist size, the same principles apply; it all starts with you.

This book will take you on a journey into your mind. You will learn the mechanics of creation, which is the first step in understanding how to apply it in your own life through the practical tips and exercises. Full disclaimer: Be prepared to discover a great deal about yourself and by default, you'll learn about others, too, which will probably answer a lot of questions you have about some people along the way. It certainly did for me!

Before you dive in, here's a quick guide on how to use this book.

As with anything in life, there are always exceptions, so if I generalise at points throughout this book, it's only to assist in understanding the message I want to get across.

I'm assuming that because you are reading this, you are ready to make changes and step up your game. For change to happen, you have to know where you are starting from.

You are going to learn a lot about yourself and other people through this process; maybe you will recognise elements of yourself in some of the stories you read.

Throughout the book, you will also find Activation Tools, which are practical tips and exercises to put your knowledge into action and begin making positive changes in your life.

My suggestion is to read the book from beginning to end and in order, as each chapter builds on the previous one and so jumping ahead may leave you a little confused.

You can carry out the exercises as you go along, or you may

prefer to read through the whole book first and then revisit the exercises in the order they appear in the book.

The best way to get results from the exercises is to answer the questions, trusting whatever comes to mind.

Allow yourself to be vulnerable and uncover some of the things that you may have been unaware of until reading this book. If you hold back, then the things you want in life will hold back, too.

You can use this book as a working manual and refer back to any chapter and the Activation Tools in them, as needed in the future.

Download an editable workbook at (website address)

Most importantly, enjoy this part of the never-ending journey of self-discovery and growth.

You may be wondering who I am and why you should listen to anything I have to say. That's a fair question.

My journey was a different kind of grind, but it led me to the exact tools that high-performers need to overcome their biggest mental roadblocks. This book is the result of that discovery. I'm an internationally certified Trainer and Master Practitioner of Neuro-Linguistic Programming, Time Line Therapy®, Hypnotherapy and an Alchemy and Breathwork facilitator.

I've since coached hundreds of people, helping them make massive shifts in their mindset and, more importantly, in their results. Everything I'll share with you is battle-tested in my own life and in the lives of my clients. This book isn't a comprehensive encyclopaedia of everything I've learned. It's the concentrated, high-impact version of what works. My promise is that if you take just one principle from this book and apply it, you could change the entire trajectory of your life.

I used to beat myself up for not having already achieved all my goals. But I've come to realise that growth isn't a finish line; it's a continuous journey. There are no limitations other than the ones we create in our minds and I'm here to show you how to recognise and rewire them.

My intention is simple: to give you the blueprint to reconstruct your mind and activate your winning formula. This isn't about eliminating challenges - they will still come. It's about building the flexibility, resilience and mindset to navigate them with ease and come out stronger.

This isn't a magic pill and that shiny red car won't just appear in your driveway tomorrow. But this book will give you the edge you've been looking for. It's time to stop leaving your success to chance and start intentionally shaping it.

With that in mind, let's begin!

1

Designing Your Reality

To be unstoppable, you must know, feel, think and take action.

Every big achievement starts as an idea – a spark in the mind before it ever becomes visible in the world. Whether it's launching a business, running a marathon, or writing a book, what eventually takes shape in the physical world is the result of something that began internally. The physical result is simply the evidence of all the work, decisions and alignment that came before it.

That's why, if you want to create physical changes, it's crucial to understand where the physical fits into the bigger equation of reality.

Think of an architect before the first brick is ever laid. The building already exists in sketches, calculations and imagination. By the time it's standing, the physical structure is just the final chapter of a much longer process.

In the same way, goals are a physical manifestation of something you've created. The physical is important, but it's only one part of the puzzle.

High-performers in every field share one trait... they know that results don't begin in the gym, the office, or the studio. They begin in the unseen layers of thought, belief and emotion. The physical outcome is just the evidence.

That's why understanding where the physical fits into reality is so important if you want to create lasting change.

There are many models and schools of thought that attempt to explain how we create results. To keep things simple, I'll share the framework that I've found most relevant and practical when pursuing any goal.

The universe and the reality you experience within it, operates across four interconnected planes: spiritual, mental, emotional and physical. Each plane has its own role, yet all of them influence one another. When one is out of alignment, it affects the others. When they're working in harmony, results flow more naturally. Think of them as the four dimensions of your performance - individually powerful, but truly transformative when integrated.

The Spiritual Plane

The term 'spiritual' in this context is simply a representation of the higher self. The higher self is *everything*; it's bigger than just us as physical human beings. It encompasses and knows all things and so all of creation happens on this plane. It's often referred to as infinite intelligence or the universe. While it can sometimes feel as if you're on an island by yourself, the opposite is true.

The Mental Plane

The mental plane is where your conscious mind resides, which is your thinking mind. The mental plane is where you set an intention to create something that doesn't currently exist in physical form. It's a powerful gateway to creation through intentional focus. It can keep us grounded through its rational perspective.

The Emotional Plane

The emotional plane is the home of your unconscious mind. It's the way you feel in any moment, be that an emotion you would call positive or negative, good or bad; either way, those emotions are all generated from your unconscious mind. The feelings we have about ourselves, others, the world, our situation and everything in it all exist on the emotional plane. The emotional plane is where the energy needed for physical creation is generated.

The Physical Plane

The physical plane is exactly that. It's the tangible existence where much of creation is evident in its physical form. Think of everything around you, from your house, car, shoes, phone, couch, plant pot, body and this book... everything you can physically grasp.

Everything is created twice - once in the mind and then in the outer world. Any goal starts with the conscious mind when you decide that you want something. The unconscious mind is responsible for the emotion behind it, the energy that creates it. On the spiritual plane of your higher self, the part of you that is all-knowing and connected to everything, the goal is already done; it exists in the quantum field of potentiality. Said differently, your desire exists energetically – your job is to align yourself with it through intention, belief, focus and action. Although it exists energetically, there is a delay in that energy taking physical form, which we will cover in more detail later on in the book.

In my experience, I've noticed that people will spend the majority of their time focused on or working on one plane more than the others, sometimes even discounting the others completely. The reason it's essential to acknowledge the existence of all four planes is that no plane is good or bad, wrong or right, better or worse than any other plane. They each have their purpose and taking all planes into account is fundamental to the results you achieve. Without doing so, issues can often arise because people spend time working on the wrong plane, particularly when attempting to solve a problem. While no single plane is inherently wrong or right, I use the word 'wrong' to highlight when a problem is addressed on a plane where it didn't originate. To truly resolve an issue, it must be addressed on the plane where it was created.

Think of it like this: if someone has problems that are physical, such as issues with money or a lack of energy from a poor diet and little sleep, first of all, they need to focus on the physical plane to make any necessary changes.

While the planes are all linked and all influence each other, it's important to identify which plane a problem originates from to resolve it. At the same time, you must ensure the other planes are in alignment. This is why all planes are both individual and collective.

This is a lesson I learned firsthand. For years, I tried to change the physical things in my life through thought alone. For example, money was a big issue for me, so I repeated the affirmation *"I attract money easily"* at least 200 times a day. The problems I was experiencing were overdue fees on my credit card, debtors sending final demands and very little money to survive on day to day. No amount of meditating was going to pay the bills. The immediate problem was a physical one; it existed on the physical plane and required physical action. In other words, picking up the phone, arranging a payment plan and getting work to pay the bills.

That was the starting point, but the other planes also required attention to make sure the action I did take was forward-focused (mental) and positive rather than fear-driven (emotional) – more to come on that later. This principle is the same across all planes.

First, let's identify which plane is the root cause of the problem.

Physical: The individual might be experiencing chronic fatigue, poor sleep, or a lack of energy due to overwork. They might also have a poor diet or neglect exercise.

Example: *"I'm exhausted all the time and I've been sleeping less than six hours a night. I can't seem to focus on anything."*

Emotional: The person could be feeling overwhelmed, anxious, or resentful from the pressure to perform. There might be a sense of emotional numbness or a feeling that their work is no longer fulfilling.

Example: *"I'm feeling so much pressure to succeed that I've lost the joy in my work. It feels like a constant struggle and I'm always worried I'll fall behind."*

Mental: The individual's thoughts might be racing, filled with self-doubt, or stuck in a loop of repetitive, unproductive thinking. They might struggle to find new ideas or feel a lack of intellectual stimulation.

Example: *"My mind is completely blank. I've been trying to solve this problem for weeks, but I feel like I'm hitting a wall. I can't generate any new ideas."*

Spiritual: The person may have lost their sense of purpose. Their work might not align with their core values anymore, or they may feel disconnected from the "why" behind their ambition.

Example: *"I've achieved everything I set out to, but I still feel empty inside. My success doesn't feel meaningful anymore and I'm questioning why I'm even doing this."*

To bring this framework to life, consider a common scenario for high-performers: a driven individual achieves a significant career milestone – a promotion, a win, or the launch of a successful project. They've taken massive physical action and produced a significant result.

Yet, they find themselves still plagued by the same old insecurities. Despite the external validation and the new title on their business card or the trophy, they feel like an imposter. They experience the same mental struggles with self-doubt and the same emotional anxiety about not being good enough. They've changed the outside, but the inside feels exactly the same.

Making physically desirable changes doesn't guarantee your

thoughts and feelings will change, too. If anything, it can add to any doubt that was already present and labels such as imposter syndrome can be added to the list of limitations.

The spiritual plane is where you hand over the outcome to something bigger than yourself – whether that's the universe, a higher power, or simply the flow of life. It's the trust that comes after you've done the work on the other three planes. You've taken the physical action, aligned your mental beliefs and managed your emotional state. The spiritual plane is where you let go of the need to control the final result and simply allow it to unfold.

At different stages of life, one plane will always demand more of your attention than the others. The goal isn't to be a perfect master of all four planes at once. Instead, the key to becoming the captain of your life is to recognise when a plane is out of balance and to work on bringing all four into harmony. When your physical, emotional, mental and spiritual planes are working together, you not only achieve success but also feel a profound sense of purpose and fulfilment.

Activation Tool – *Checking Your Alignment*

Take an area of life you want to improve or a problem you want to resolve.

Ask yourself the following questions:

On which plane does the root of this problem exist?

- Spiritual (higher self) – greater than and encompassing everyone and everything
- Mental – thinking
- Emotional – feelings
- Physical – tangible substance or matter

For example,

Person A:

"I want to lose weight, but I don't do any exercise and I often eat fast food because it's quick and easy." (Physical)

Person B:

"I go to the gym and keep active, but I eat to make me feel good." (Emotional)

If I were to focus on one plane, which would have the most significant impact first?

Person A: Physical

"Starting with this will have immediate results."

Person B: Emotional

"Dealing with my emotions will stop the overeating and the physical effort will begin to pay off."

Attempting to change everything at once can very quickly become overwhelming and the very thing that needs addressing can easily be overlooked. By identifying which plane the problem exists on, you can begin to break it down and deal with it, one step at a time.

Working on the plane where the problem exists will usually have a positive knock-on effect on the other planes, too. Any real change is uncomfortable; if it weren't, then everyone would be doing it. If you're not sure where to begin, check which plane you've been avoiding. This will most likely be an indication of discomfort and is often where the magic lies.

2

The Immutable Rules of Achievement

"Take away the cause and the effect ceases."
Miguel de Cervantes

We are very soon going to be getting into the nitty-gritty of you and your RAS, but stick with me for just a little while longer first.

In the wonderful place we know as the universe, along with the four planes – physical, mental, emotional and spiritual – there are also seven primary natural laws, or principles, that act as a framework by which the universe operates. Understanding these laws, which planes they exist on and how you can utilise them is the foundation of your existence.

Of these seven universal laws, there are some that are much more well-known and spoken about than others. However, in isolation, much of their power is lost. These laws are present and happening at all times; you cannot turn them off or pick and choose which ones you will use and when. They all have an impact on your results and your ability to become an expert creator in your life, so understanding them is a key part of understanding yourself.

I won't be going into any great detail in this book; there are many resources you can find on this topic if you want to know more. I have listed some in the Resources section at the back of this book. However, you will become aware of the laws' existence and how you can purposefully use them to make positive changes in your life.

Let's explain the whole 'law' thing first. To simplify this idea, consider the Law of Gravity. Everyone knows and accepts that what goes up must come down. Knowing the Law of Gravity exists influences how you behave and the choices you make. For instance, you probably choose the stairs rather than stepping out of a second-floor bedroom window when leaving the house, because in knowing the Law of Gravity, you accept that the second-floor window option may not end well. It also gives you peace of mind that when a child jumps high in the air on a bouncy castle, you can sit and watch, safe in the knowledge that they will eventually come back down again.

What you need to be aware of here is that gravity is neither good nor bad and the same is true for everything else in life. Nothing that exists is good or bad, nor does it have any meaning, other than the meaning you give it. Assuming you can defy the laws is like throwing an apple in the air and hoping it will never come back down again. If you're not careful, you may well get hit in the face by a falling apple... Better to use your knowledge and the laws to your advantage and work in harmony with them!

Immutable or mutable? That is the question...

Each law falls into one of two categories: immutable or mutable. Sounds fancy, right?

The immutable laws are the first three laws and quite simply, they are laws that are fixed - they cannot be changed.

Immutable Laws

- Law of Mentalism
- Law of Correspondence
- Law of Vibration

The mutable laws are the other four laws and these laws can be changed or transcended.

Mutable Laws

- Law of Polarity
- Law of Rhythm
- Law of Cause and Effect
- Law of Gender

The principles all link and work together to create this thing we call life. Learning the basics will give you some insight, not only into yourself but also into the bigger picture at play and the impact it has on you personally.

* * *

Immutable Laws

Law #1: Law of Mentalism

"The universe is mental, held in the mind of THE ALL."

Put another way, the mind is all; the universe is mental!

The universe is the source of all things and those 'things' include you. ALL is everything that exists, the universe itself, everything you could ever think of... I mean *everything.* Every single one of us is born from the same source, which means we all have that source within us.

The 'all' literally contains everything and so nothing exists outside of it, before it or after it. It is the whole, so you are part of the universe and the universe is part of you.

The law states that the mind is all, which means that everything that is created is also your mind.

Stick with me here!

The universe is mental; therefore, everything is created through the mind. Every single thing that ever has or ever will exist starts and is experienced in the mind first.

Your physical reality is a reflection of your mental reality.

If the whole universe is mental, then reality is not an external experience – it's all internal. In other words, your reality exists in your mind and you can create your own experience of it. This also means you are the only one who can change it. Now that may sound a bit scary: *"Oh crap, I'm in charge of my entire life!"*.

Well, here's the thing... Because you are the only one in control of your reality, that means you're already doing it, so you may as well do it on purpose!

Your entire existence all happens through your mind, so anything you have the capacity to think, you also can create... Starting to sound more like fun?

The thing that stops people from creating what they want is their beliefs, emotions and perceptions of what something is. As A. Victor Segno wrote in 'The Law of Mentalism,'

"All things exist, but man knows of them only so far as he is educated to comprehend them. What is a fact to one is an unreality to another; thus, no two people will exactly agree upon a given subject."

Think of it like this: we can all agree that rain, in and of itself, has no meaning. Yet, to a farmer, it could fill them with joy knowing their crops will be watered. A small child, on the other hand, could be sad because they can no longer go out to play at the park. A farmer may find his crops flooded from the downpour and a child could play for hours splashing in puddles.

There is no good or bad in life; it's all about perspective!

The mind creates everything and you are part of everything, so you have the power to do, be or have anything. There is no physical path that isn't first born in the mind. This is where the energy is created – in the mental.

Slightly mind-bending, hey?

The key point to all of this is to know that you are the one in control of your own mind! No one can make you think anything unless you choose to and understanding this is a great starting point to mastering your thoughts.

Everything that is created in the physical plane is mental first. Without a thought of a table, a table would not exist and therefore, it would not be able to become a physical thing. The focus or intention of your observation changes your reality. If you're not focusing on something in your world, then does it even exist? Focus is powerful when it comes to choosing the direction of your life, so I highly recommend that you begin to become aware of what you are placing your attention and focus on.

The joy of creation comes from bringing thoughts from the mental plane into the physical, which requires action. Many people resist this part as it's much easier to sit and think about what you want than it is to pursue something new and often uncomfortable.

As with everything, there is, of course, the flip side - in this case, it can be that people spend their whole time being physical, pursuing their lives with brute force, taking non-stop action without ever attending to what's happening on the mental plane, in their minds.

The mind is what creates the will to act (mental); action needs to then be taken (physical). Not tending to the mental can certainly make physical action feel like an uphill battle. When the mental is in alignment, the physical follows far more easily.

If your goal is to be the best in your industry, you need to take action. Any action is generated in the mind first.

Use the Law of Mentalism to clear the mental path; create what you want mentally first. The Law of Mentalism allows you to zoom out your perspective and see that you are part of a much bigger picture and so much more connected and powerful than you know.

Activation Tool - Applying the Law of Mentalism

Begin to become aware of your thoughts and notice any limiting beliefs or negative emotions you have that could prevent you from achieving your outcomes. Any limitations in the mind will become evident in the physical.

You can use the following questions as prompts:

- **What beliefs do I have that could prevent me from achieving my goals?**
- **When I consider what I want, what emotions and beliefs are associated with it?**

Write down whatever comes to mind, even if it doesn't make any sense at this point.

Once completed, go through each belief and emotion and ask yourself the following questions:

- **How would I know if that belief wasn't true? What would have to happen?**
- **If the emotion disappeared right now, what did I learn from the events that created it?**

Every obstacle is simply a perception – the bigger we perceive it to be, the bigger the lesson we take from it. Just considering these questions will begin to turn you towards overcoming those limitations. Good job!

* * *

Law #2: Law of Correspondence

"As above, so below. As within, so without."

The Law of Correspondence is the principle that you are totally in control of your experience.

Remember, we live in a world that exists on different planes: the physical plane, which is matter (the earth-bound stuff); then there is the mental plane, which is your mind and consciousness; the emotional plane, which is your unconscious mind; and finally, the spiritual plane, which is where you have access to your higher consciousness.

There is a correspondence between each of the planes, which means the experiences that you have on one plane are a direct reflection of what is happening on the other planes, too. There is nothing in your external experience that isn't happening in your internal experience – the planes are a mirror image of each other.

If a change takes place on the physical plane, there must also be a change happening on the mental plane. If you shift the physical, there has to be a shift on the mental, as they correspond with each other; they are both evolving at the same time.

To bring this to life, imagine we have Person A and Person B. Person A wants to do good and *"save the world"*, whereas Person B prefers to spend their time complaining about how rubbish the world is and everything in it. As someone looking in, you would probably assume the internal worlds of Person A and Person B are very different and they will be because no two people ever have the same experience of the world, but either way, both people see the world as being broken in some form. They both see a world that needs fixing, improving or saving.

If we apply the Law of Correspondence to this situation, when someone sees the world as needing to be saved or fixed, this will be a reflection of what is happening internally for that person. It may be that they feel broken in some way or like they need saving.

The way to change how you see the world and to really save it is to save yourself, because everything is a reflection of you. What is happening on the inside, your thoughts and feelings, is what determines everything outside of you. Remember, this works both ways, as each plane corresponds with the others. When the things you take in from the outside change, the inside will also change, so start to become mindful of how you spend your time and who you spend it with.

Be aware of what you feed your body, the physical part of you, as it will always impact the other planes. This also applies to what you feed your mind and your spirit, which, of course, correspond with your physical experience. What happens on one plane also occurs on the 'ALL'.

You are part of the universe (the above) and the universe is within you (the below).

The Law of Correspondence is such an important law and it links the three immutable laws together.

Activation Tool – Applying the Law of Correspondence

Begin to use your experience of your external world as feedback by reflecting it back on yourself. This relates to both the wanted and the unwanted.

If there is something you want to change, ask yourself the following questions and trust what comes to mind.

· **What is it within me that's causing this external experience?**

Notice the words you use and turn them inwards.

If the world outside of you is filled with lack, scarcity or helplessness, then ask where in yourself you feel those things.

· **What do I need to change in myself so the reflection outside of me changes?**

Remember, the outside is a reflection of you and you are a reflection of it. When you know the cause of your life events, you can choose whether or not you want to change them.

· **What am I feeding myself, mentally and physically?**

Our physical behaviour can often fall out of our awareness

without us even noticing. This could include the food you eat, exercise, sleep, meditation, relaxation, relationships, who you spend your time with, the activities you do, TV shows you watch, books you read, conversations you have... and any other areas that affect your mental and physical well-being.

Make a note of how you spend your time and with whom and notice how you feel when you do. If something, or someone, isn't serving you, maybe it's time to let it go.

· **What positive changes can I make to my body and mind?**

Decide what you will do instead. Making small changes adds up to big changes over time. Pick one or two and do those first before starting on the next. The small wins will soon build up.

This is exciting! Trying to change the world never works - there are too many things outside of your control. The only thing you can change is you and when you do, the world you see will change.

"Be the change you wish to see in the world."
   Gandhi

* * *

Law #3: Law of Vibration

"Nothing rests, everything moves, everything vibrates."
"Energy is everything and everything is energy."

This is the language of energy and the foundation of the Law of Attraction, a secondary law that operates on the principle that vibration is what causes attraction. The Law of Vibration states that everything that exists is vibrating; nothing stands still. Whilst this may not appear to be the case when you're looking at a pretty sturdy table, if you were to put that table under a microscope (albeit a very big one), you'd see that it is actually moving.

From a metaphysical perspective, energy is the core of everything, even things that appear solid. The very sturdy table you see is a manifestation of energy vibrating at a frequency that makes it appear in its solid form. Scientists state that all things in the universe are made of particles, which are tiny pieces of matter. Those particles are energy travelling in wave form and the up-and-down sequence - just like the waves on a heart rate monitor rise and fall, waves of energy in the universe also move in patterns and each wave varies. The variation is what determines the form the energy takes and, therefore, the object that you perceive in front of you. Whilst you can't see particles vibrating, they are the very things keeping the sturdy items that you can touch in place.

Think of it like a guitar string being plucked. The frequency at which the string vibrates determines the sounds that are produced; this is the same for all matter and physical creation.

The frequency of the vibration is the only difference between our physical body and the 'ALL'. Matter has a lower frequency, so the more solid something is, the slower the particles are moving and the slower the speed or rate of vibration. The faster the vibration of the particles, the more energy-based and less tangible the physical form.

The frequency of the vibration is the number of wave cycles per second. Because everything is energy, there is no difference between you and the material stuff outside of you; it's just a different frequency. Changing the frequency of vibration changes the experience in the physical form. As humans, we are also vibrating, constantly. The only variable is the rate we vibrate at, which is determined by how we feel.

The physical world is focused thought, focused vibration and this is true of you, too. Everything that exists in the physical began as a thought. The more focus you give to a thought, whether positive or negative, the more focused it becomes and it then matches the experiences, the people and outcomes that are equal to it.

Whether it's a big idea, a promotion, winning the competition, or anything else, you can only bring it to fruition in a sustainable way when you're able to handle it. Your inner world – your thoughts, beliefs, memories and emotions – determines your frequency and whether or not you have the capacity to hold your desires. Striving for something you believe you don't deserve will limit or at least slow down the likelihood of it happening.

On the flip side, you can be a match to things that have not yet made their way into your experience, but they are coming!

Remember, the Law of Correspondence states that if things change on one plane, the other planes must correspond to and be a reflection of that. If there are changes to your vibration on the mental and emotional plane, the physical plane must correspond.

It's worth mentioning here that there is a time lag between the mental and the physical, so whilst the things you think about may not immediately fall out of the sky, they are in the formation process. Think of it like the birth of a baby. No one expects a baby to be ready to go after three months of pregnancy. There is a nine-month gestation period, when the baby is making its way into physical form. Whilst there is no set time frame for a thought to make its way into your world, there is a gestation period where the energy is taking form and so the same law applies.

The question is, how can you become a match to the things you desire?

And, how long does it take for the metaphorical baby to be born - for thoughts to become tangible?

We'll get to that soon! To truly be a purposeful creator, it's important to understand how it works first so you can replicate the process every time!

Activation Tool – Applying the Law of Vibration

You're already becoming aware of your thoughts through your application of the Law of Mentalism. It's time to take it a step further. Your thoughts influence the way you feel.

- **Notice the feelings that are associated with the thoughts you have – how do the thoughts feel?**
- **When you have a good feeling out of the blue, become aware of what you were thinking about?**

You'll have identified some thoughts that feel good and some that don't feel so good. Awareness is key when making any change – you can't change what you don't know exists. We'll talk more about what to do with any thoughts that feel negative or don't support you later on.

- **Decide to focus daily on the 'good feeling' thoughts.**

Take just a few minutes a day to sit and really get into the details of each thought. Become aware of what you can see in your mind, what sounds are present, the feelings, smells or tastes. As you notice all of those finer details, allow the good feelings to become more intense. Then, let these feelings spread throughout your body.

Start with just a few minutes and if you want to, stay there longer. This exercise should be fun, so do it for the sheer pleasure of it and enjoy the process!

To summarise the immutable, unchangeable laws:

· The Law of Mentalism

The mind is the 'ALL'; the universe is mental (the mind), so therefore you are everything and everything is you.

· The Law of Correspondence

You are the 'ALL' and the 'ALL' is everything, so the four planes of existence – physical, mental, emotional and spiritual – that make up your being, are all one. When one changes, the others must correspond.

· The Law of Vibration

Everything is energy and vibrates at a certain frequency. The universe is mental and you are part of it. Your thoughts and feelings emit at a frequency rate that dictates the physical things that show up outside of you. As your internal frequency changes, so does your external reality. You are in the 'ALL,' and the physical manifestation must correspond.

* * *

Mutable Laws

Law #4: Law of Polarity

"Everything exists in duality, everything has poles, everything has its opposite. However, opposites are identical in their nature and different only in degree."

Everything is one thing that is expressed in two ways: a positive and a negative, or a masculine and a feminine energy, although not necessarily related to gender. It's important to note that the word 'positive' in this context doesn't mean better; batteries have a positive and a negative charge that work together. When it comes to creation, there will always be something that is wanted and then its polar opposite, the unwanted.

For everything that exists, there will be an opposite end of the scale: light and dark, loud and quiet, rich and poor, happy and sad. Everything is dual.

To understand how two things are expressed as one, think about it in terms of hot and cold. Whilst hot and cold are opposites, they are also varying degrees of the same thing – temperature. This is where the saying, 'there is a thin line between love and hate,' comes from; they're both on the same scale. The law is relative to each person – what you think of as being at one end of the pole, another person may see further down, as a lesser degree.

There is a duality in everything; opposites are an illusion!

There are two ends of everything – the wanted and the un-wanted. They may look like opposites, but they are simply two expressions of the same spectrum. One cannot exist without the other – it's the law. What appears to be two opposites is really just one thing expressed in different degrees.

The reason this is so important is that if you reject one end of the pole, you're inadvertently rejecting the other end too. If you resist failure – rejecting it, fearing it, or refusing to accept its possibility - you also resist success. Success and failure are two ends of the same spectrum and by pushing one away, you unintentionally block the other. You narrow down your window of tolerance to either extreme – the consequence is a life of mediocracy. When you become okay with both, knowing you can handle whatever comes, you expand your capacity to navigate challenges and opportunities alike.

Duality is a fact of life - struggle and success go hand in hand. The challenges you face are often the conditions required for growth and the absence of what you want defines its value – this is where desires are born!

Let's face it, there's nothing quite like losing or underperforming to highlight what you don't want! This is a great starting point to direct and sharpen your focus toward what is wanted!

Activation Tool – Applying the Law of Polarity

Start appreciating the experiences you have had to date, especially the ones that, until now, you may have seen as bad, pointless or a waste of time. Without them, you wouldn't be aware of their opposites.

Ask yourself the following questions:

· **What is the polar opposite of the things I don't want?**

If you're experiencing a 'bad patch', be that in relationships, your career, health or any other area, use it as data, showing you the end of the scale. Take peace in knowing that your awareness of it has served a purpose and without it, your desires wouldn't exist either. Then use the clarity it brings to turn your aim towards what is wanted.

· **What does your life look, sound and feel like when you are living that experience? Write down your answer in as much detail as you can.**

Do this exercise from a place of enjoyment. You now know the opposite end of the scale to where you currently, or don't want to, exist, so indulge in it. The mental plane corresponds with the physical, so start mentally creating the reality you desire.

There is one place where duality does not exist: the spiritual plane, because on the spiritual plane, everything is one. When you decide to rise above judgment or the labelling of things as being either good or bad – whether that's thoughts, feelings, people, circumstances or events – you don't become attached to either extreme of the scale. You're then able to see either side of any situation as being different expressions of the same thing.

Accepting where you are now as the gift it truly is, this is the first step to creating its opposite. Polarity is the gift of clarity!

* * *

Law #5: Law of Rhythm

"Everything flows, everything has its tides, all things rise and fall, a pendulum that swings to the right swings to the left in equal measure, what goes up must come down, rhythm compensates."

The Law of Rhythm applies to everything in life. Waves that come in must go back out. Day is always followed by night and night is followed by day. When there is a downfall in the economy, it's followed by a boom. These are the natural rhythms of life and for every high, there will be an equal low.

"The measure of the swing to the right is the measure of the swing to the left; rhythm compensates."

Let's use a pendulum to demonstrate how the law works: when it swings in one direction, by law, it has to then swing back in the opposite direction to compensate. It doesn't swing one way and then just come back to the centre and stop and this same law is also true in life. If things are exceptionally great, they flow easily – you feel wonderful, have loads of energy and life feels easy. Then, by law, this will be followed by days when everything feels difficult and rubbish for no reason at all. The same tasks that felt easy to do one week can feel like there is a bag of cement attached to them the next! This applies to everything, to all areas of life, from health and relationships to career, money and all others.

Everything flows up and down, so there will always be a corresponding peak for every trough. This is so important to grasp because it can give you a sense of peace, knowing that when things aren't great and the pendulum of life has swung in the direction of the unwanted, where life feels hard, you can rest assured that it's not forever. The Law of Rhythm is at work and so it will swing back to where life feels good again. The way to utilise this law is to accept that when the lows happen, no matter how far down they may pull you, they are temporary. Holding this in mind is such a gift during those times and can help you stay focused on what you want, no matter what.

Working with this law is how you can create balance – by avoiding the very high highs followed by the very low lows. The more balanced you are on the scale, the less swing there will be in either direction. This doesn't mean avoiding highs altogether; it's about finding a balance through both the ups and the downs. Rather than living life at extremes, from obsessive or overly excited to completely depressed, look for the opposite in each of them to create harmony.

This law is evident in high-performers – there have been many cases of celebrities or athletes at their peak, soaking up the crowd's applause, only to be followed by such a huge crash that they resort to drugs, alcohol, or other methods in an attempt to lift themselves out of the low. This can create an inner resistance to achieving their goals – even if it's what they really want, the fear of being able to handle all of it can appear to be too high a price to pay and the body responds accordingly – you energetically push away your desires.

So when things are really great and you feel like jumping around like an enthusiastic bunny shouting from the rooftops, find calm and peace within that. If you find yourself feeling obsessed by something, seek out other things you can do to steady your attention. This will prevent the pendulum from going so far in one direction and, therefore, having to swing back in equal measure. The more stable and neutral you are mentally and emotionally, regardless of external circumstances, the more your body - the nervous system - can handle without crashing. This opens up your capacity to experience the more extreme moments without the negative consequences that often follow.

Activation Tool – Applying the Law of Rhythm

When you experience a super high moment in your life, normalise it by finding the calm and peace within you while simultaneously enjoying your experience.

- **Create a list of things that ground you so you have them available to put into practice without having to think about it.**

This could be something as simple as taking a bath, meditating, walking in nature or doing something positive to help someone who has less than you.

When you experience a moment that is on the lower end of the feel-good scale, it's essential to keep focused on your goal, even if it seems impossible to achieve in that moment. There's nothing inherently wrong or bad about any low; it's just the resistance to the feeling that makes it feel as though there is.

- **Make a list of all the things that are within your control (there may only be a few!).**

Only work on the things from your list; forget about everything else beyond that, which will usually be outside of your control anyway.

When the pendulum has swung in the direction where you don't feel so good, keep things really simple. Attempting to do too much can very quickly become overwhelming and lead to feeling even worse. Relax knowing that this too shall pass. Ironically, the more accepting you become, the better you will feel and, as a result, the quicker it passes.

* * *

Law #6: Law of Cause and Effect

"Every cause has an effect, every effect has its cause and every action has its reaction."

This law states that there are no accidents in life. Everything that exists within your reality – whether you deem it good or bad, wanted or unwanted – is a consequence of the thoughts and actions that preceded it; nothing happens by chance.

This law is really about taking full responsibility for your life, understanding that wherever you are right now, wherever you have found yourself, is the result of the choices you have made so far. Of course, there will have been times in the past when you had little control over experiences, yet what you always have control over is how you respond to them and how you choose to use those experiences to create what happens in the future.

Think of cause and effect like an equation: the cause equals the effect that follows, or, for every effect that happens, there is something that caused it. There are two sides to the equation and we get to choose which one to operate from and live our lives from. A life on the cause side is one where you accept that every effect that happens was, is and always will be caused by you. It's taking FULL responsibility for all of your life, which is the only way you can really make changes to it.

This may not sound appealing. It can be uncomfortable at times, but it's also the most empowering!

Life on the effect side of the equation is a life of blame, reasons and excuses about why things aren't the way you want them to be, whether it's because of age, having children, the economy, time, lack of education, an unhappy upbringing, the wrong hair colour, being too short, too tall... the list goes on!

This way of living is highly encouraged by society and it keeps people stuck in their problems. Whilst it may appear easier to blame the world and everyone in it for how your life has turned out, it's giving your power away, taking your energy with it.

Living life at effect is the quickest way to have no influence over how it turns out – you become powerless to cause any change. This is leaving things to fate rather than acknowledging that it's up to you to be in the driving seat of your own life.

Although it can seem more comfortable, relinquishing all responsibility for your life is actually really hard. This creates a life that happens to people and with it comes all the external reasons why things aren't the way they want them to be. The first obstacle that presents itself is a great excuse to give up. If everyone used their circumstances as the reason why things are the way they are, then we would undoubtedly live in a world with little achievement.

The famous psychiatrist, Carl Jung, once said:

"Until you make the unconscious conscious, it will direct your life and you will call it fate."

Making the unconscious conscious is about becoming aware

of your own patterns, often running on repeat - the thoughts you have, the behaviours you carry out and assessing whether the effect they are producing is what you want. If not, it's time to change them.

This law can also be used as a feedback mechanism. The cause, or the input, creates the effect, or the result. If you're not sure what you've been thinking and how you've been behaving until now, you can reverse engineer what is and isn't working by looking at the results you have, the effects of your current input. Use this information to determine what caused the result. And if it's not supporting you in reaching your goals, you can work out what needs to change.

The Law of Cause and Effect exists on all four planes of existence: the spiritual, the emotional, the mental and the physical.

On the spiritual plane, cause and effect happen instantly and so it can appear that cause and effect are not separate from each other. On the other planes, we have the concept of time and space and so this creates a time delay between the onset of the cause and the effect that eventually follows. For example, on the physical plane, it's accepted that, over time, eating certain foods or doing specific exercises will affect a person's weight and health.

Food/Exercise (cause) = Weight/Health (effect)

If the effect you currently have is unwanted, change the cause and the effect has to change too.

49

When your desires have a focused intention driving them, they are automatically created on the spiritual plane and the saying 'as above, so below' means that the physical reality must follow in time; that is, unless you change the input to something that contradicts it. Conflicting input will lead to inconsistent results.

A life at effect is a life of regret. You only have to imagine yourself taking your last breath with a long list of reasons and excuses as to why it wasn't the life you could've had to know this is true. There is no reason or excuse significant enough to not live a life wholeheartedly pursuing your dreams!

Activation Tool – Applying the Law of Cause and Effect

To create something new or different, you must first become aware that it exists by making it conscious and then take responsibility for changing it.

Become aware of your thoughts, feelings and behaviours as these are what will cause the effects that follow.

- **Every evening, write down what happened that day that was outside of your control and your response to it.**

Putting things outside of your control means it's outside of your control to change them.

· **Choose to take responsibility.**

Acknowledge that you cannot always change the external circumstances or people in them. The only thing you can change is you and that is your responsibility, no one else's.

· **Choose where you would like to make changes and adapt your response next time. Decide what you will do instead that puts you in the driving seat.**

Only then can you make changes. Just pretend you are responsible for EVERYTHING that happens in your life, even if you don't quite believe it yet.

· **Change the word 'can't' to the word 'won't'.**

This simple shift makes a massive difference. It turns what you do or don't do into a choice, putting you in control.

It also allows you to forget about the things you're not doing, rather than creating a vicious cycle of *"I can't do it,"* shortly followed by *"I should've done it,"* which can then lead to *"I'm such a failure."*

Instead of going through all the reasons and excuses why you 'can't' do things, accept responsibility that you 'won't' do them – because they are not as important as other things right now and that's okay. It's your choice and that is empowering!

* * *

Law #7: Law of Gender

"Gender is in everything; everything has its masculine and feminine principles; gender manifests on all planes."

The Law of Gender is not about gender itself; it's about masculine and feminine energy, both of which are found in everything.

Feminine energy expresses itself through intuition, love, care and gentleness. It flows from your unconscious mind, where your emotions reside. This is true in nature, hence the term 'mother nature'. Feminine energy is the newness of life, being impregnated, quite literally, on the physical plane and also with new ideas. It's where creativity is born.

Masculine energy is linear, a directed, focused energy where intentions are set and carried out. It's the energy of getting stuff done!

To create the life you desire, it's crucial to have a balance of the two energies. Many people get stuck in one or the other at different times in their lives.

The female is the receiver and the male is the director, a powerful combination!

Let me explain. The feminine part of your mind is where you receive ideas and inspiration, where everything is given birth to. Whilst you need feminine energy for the creation process, the energy itself has no specific aim – it's flowing all over the place. Masculine energy then directs those ideas to bring them into existence through focus and will. To maximise the potential of your own mind, you need to have both parts working together.

Be aware that if you don't utilise your own masculine energy, you won't be the one directing your life and if you're not the one doing it, that means someone else is. Those who are mentally strong-willed have a lot of masculine energy, which influences those who haven't tapped into their own.. This is why many people end up taking on the energy of whoever they are following at that time, whether that's someone speaking on the latest podcast, at an event or training, colleagues, friends or anyone else who has a strong masculine energy. They end up channelling that person's energy rather than learning how to work with their own.

When you allow yourself to let go of what you think about the world, who you are, the structures and belief systems you have taken on, you release the resistance of trying to be, do or have what you think you 'should'.

The clearer and more open you are to being the true version of you, the easier it is to tap into your own source energy to come up with your own ideas. Taking those ideas and writing them down gives you focus so you can channel your masculine power to start making them a reality.

There are standards that people impose upon themselves as a measure of their own success – the relationship, the education, the house, the car, the holidays – and hey, if those are the things you desire, great. That's okay! The point is that throughout the whole of the country you live in, even the world, there really is no way that almost every single person wants exactly the same things, yet so many strive for the same results.

If nothing more, I encourage you to take the time to be really honest with yourself about whether you are being true to yourself or allowing the masculine energy outside of you to influence your direction. If you're going to spend time working on intentionally creating your life, it may as well be one that you want, rather than what others say you should have.

Activation Tool – Applying the Law of Gender

Time to be honest with yourself!

- **If comparison didn't exist and no one would ever know what you did or didn't do, had, or didn't have, what is it you truly desire?**

Allow yourself to answer this fully by putting pen to paper, answering them as though no one is watching, so you can be you.

This is an important step because a goal born out of necessity, rather than true desire, lacks meaning. If it's something you believe you *should* want, rather than something you genuinely do, resistance will surface - and you may unconsciously sabotage your progress without understanding why.

· **Notice where you spend the majority of your time. Are you constantly taking action and pushing, using your will? Or do you go with the flow, letting your inspiration guide you with very little action?**

Of course, you may be doing a mixture of both, but you will usually find that you favour one over the other.

Consider where you may benefit from balancing your energy to utilise both masculine and feminine.

· **Allow time for creativity, self-care and inspiration, embracing your feminine energy whilst also using your masculine energy for direction and focus when taking action.**

Remember, you have both masculine and feminine energy within you and working together with both in partnership gives you access to the divine feminine of birth and creation of ideas, as well as the masculine to bring those ideas into the physical world.

So that's just a brief overview of the universal laws and

how they relate to your world. I invite and encourage you to keep them in mind at all times. Refer back to them to check if there is a law you haven't been practising or haven't considered. Use them as a guide whilst, at the same time, not being at the effect of them. The laws aren't to blame for the situations you find yourself in, so using them as the reason why you haven't achieved what you want would be putting responsibility outside of you and ignoring the Law of Cause and Effect.

The laws are always at play, just like the Law of Gravity, so working with them is one way to begin to construct the life you want.

3

Reprogramming the 95%

"In a very real sense, we have two minds, one that thinks and one that feels."
Daniel Goleman

Many years ago, I worked with a coaching client who couldn't understand why, despite all his talent and discipline, he kept derailing the very things he said he wanted. For confidentiality, we'll call him *James*.

James had a pattern, subtle but consistent, of sabotaging anything that brought him closer to the success he craved.

I remember one of our sessions when he told me about the night before a major competition. Everything was in place, yet he found himself restless and agitated, convinced something was off. By the end of the evening, he'd talked himself into changing a key part of his routine at the last minute, something he'd practised for months, only to regret it the moment it was done. He knew it wasn't logical, but he couldn't stop himself and that's the point of unconscious patterns. He said, *"It's like there's this part of me that steps in right before the breakthrough and quietly pulls me back... and I don't know why."*

"It was the night before the first major event of the season − the one everything funnels into. I'd trained, prepared and hit every target. The team was confident. I should've been, too. But alone in the hotel room, the silence was louder than it should've been.

My gear was already set out. My notes had been reviewed twice, maybe three times, but I wasn't really taking them in anymore. Instead, I found myself staring out the window, tapping my fingers against the armrest, as if I was waiting for something to go wrong.

It's always like this the night before. Not nerves exactly. More like a hum under the surface −restless, agitated, like part of me is on edge without knowing why.

I caught myself thinking about last season and those key moments I don't usually like to admit to anyone - the small hesitations. The times I held back just slightly. Nothing obvious. Nothing you could pick up on unless you really knew how I worked. At the time, I convinced myself it was a strategy. That I was being smart, not reckless. But now, I'm not so sure.

I can feel it creeping in again - this subtle urge to adjust, second-guess, delay. To play it a little safer. A little smaller. Like if I edge back just enough, I can avoid the fallout if things go wrong. Or worse - if they go right.

And I know I'm doing it. That's the most frustrating part. I'm aware of the pattern. I can see the thoughts as they start. But I don't know why they're there. I don't want to mess this up. I don't want to fall short. And yet... here I am, rehearsing how to shrink without looking like I did. It's as if I find new ways to trip myself up right when it matters most.

The crazy part is that I really want this, so feeling this way makes no sense. The more I try to shut down any negativity, the stronger it seems to become.

James isn't alone. I've seen this pattern show up in many high-performers - driven, focused, outwardly composed - but inwardly tangled in a quiet tug-of-war between desire and doubt. It's rarely dramatic. It creeps in subtly. A hesitation. A decision slightly off-course. A moment of withdrawal disguised as control.

The desire is there, but the more he resisted his emotions, the stronger they became - an inner fight with no clear winner.

It probably comes as no surprise that rational thinking goes out of the window when it comes to emotions. You can try as much as you like, but when emotions are high, thinking like a reasoned person rarely happens easily, if at all.

It can sometimes feel as though your inner world has many different characters or, to put it another way, it can feel like you have a split personality. You're thinking one thing, but the way you feel is in total opposition and whilst you may know that, rationally, the way you feel doesn't make any sense at all, but you still feel it.

Take a breath! You can rest assured that you are completely sane... even though I know first-hand that the evidence can make you feel otherwise at times.

We're going to touch on the mechanics of your internal world and how it operates, which is the key to beginning to take control of your external world.

Conscious and Unconscious

To explain this fascinating phenomenon of how we operate as humans, I'd like to introduce you to your mind or, to be more accurate, your two minds!

I want to be clear, you only have one physical mind, but for the purpose of explaining how the mind operates, imagine having two minds living in the same space. Both minds have distinctive roles and those roles have very different functions, but both are equally important. Having an insight into the difference between them can help you identify which mind to work with to make positive changes and deal with issues when they present themselves along the way.

Say hello to your conscious and unconscious mind.

You may well have heard of them both many times before, but I'm going to go through an overview of their roles and functions in a way that will bring them to life, so you can become more familiar with them as you progress through the following chapters.

The following information is based on the study of Neuro-Linguistic Programming (NLP), developed in the 1970s by Richard Bandler and John Grinder. NLP is the study of how our brains process and interpret information, which results in the thoughts we think and our feelings, which leads to our behaviour and, ultimately, the results we get.

To give you a metaphor that will assist you with this, I want you to think of your conscious mind as a rowing boat, floating on the surface of a large ocean and your unconscious mind as a submarine under the water, with the two of them tied together by a piece of rope.

When a person wants to change direction in life, to metaphorically head towards a new destination, they will usually put all their effort into turning the rowing boat around by rowing harder and faster. The problem with this is that the submarine is still pulling in the original direction, the opposite way. If I had to place a bet on whether the rowing boat or the submarine would win, I know where I would put my money! Fighting a submarine would be hard work for anyone.

The submarine, your unconscious mind, is responsible for and drives approximately a whopping 95% of what you do or don't do. That leaves the remaining 5%, which is the rowing boat – your conscious mind. Your conscious mind is only responsible for 5% of your thoughts, feelings and the actions you take.

61

When you think of it like that, I'm sure you can appreciate why working hard in your rowing boat can feel like you're doing a lot but getting nowhere fast.

Before we dive underwater to the submarine, where you'll get to know your unconscious mind, let's get acquainted with what's on top of the water, the rowing boat – your conscious mind and the role it plays.

Your Conscious Mind

According to *Oxford Living Dictionaries*, the word 'consciousness' by definition means *"the state of being aware of and responsive to one's surroundings"*, or *"a person's awareness or perception of something"*. Consciousness is basically everything you are conscious of or aware of.

Your conscious mind is located in the left hemisphere of your brain; it's your logical thinking brain, where you rationalise and make sense of things. This is the mind that James was using to try to convince himself that he was being irrational, because his feelings made no logical sense.

As you go about your everyday, you are consciously aware of your surroundings and your experience within them. You take your world – all the things you can see, hear, feel, taste and smell – in through your five senses. Every second of every single day, everything that happens outside of you, literally everything, is being taken in through your senses, yet so much of that information is outside of your conscious awareness.

Follow along with this exercise for a moment so you can experience it for yourself:

Pause for a moment and take in just a few of the things you can see, hear, feel, smell and taste. How many things do you notice?

Now spread your awareness even further and become aware of the sounds in the distance, the feeling of your left small toe, the temperature of your skin, the feeling of the ground beneath you, your breath as it goes in and out, your right kneecap, the people passing by, the noise of the cars, the smell of next-door's food cooking or their dog barking, all the things that are the colour brown around you.

These things have always been there, but you probably haven't noticed them. In your reality, they didn't exist because you were busy focusing on other things. That was until they were brought into your conscious awareness. Of course, our physical bodies go everywhere we do, so on some level, we know they're there, but the same principle applies to the things happening outside of us, too. The things you are aware of in any moment are the things you are focusing on. As soon as you change your focus to something new, you are no longer thinking about those other things anymore.

The power of focus is what allows you to really home in on what you are doing, dismissing everything else that is going on around you. Your conscious mind, by its very nature, has a very narrow, laser-like focus because of its capacity to only hold a small amount of information at any one time. Even when its focus is only held on a particular thing for a split second, it will be solely on it in that single moment. When you train yourself to focus your attention in the right direction – in other words, on what you want – your conscious mind can be hugely powerful in helping you achieve it, if you use it in the way it was intended.

"What consumes your mind controls your life."
  Anonymous proverb

When your awareness locks onto one thing, you can become consciously consumed by it. The tunnel-like vision that it provides you with, if you choose to tap into it, is the very thing that makes some people successful in ways that many only dream of. It is the ability to block out any conflicting information and create a path of certainty inside oneself.

Of course, as with anything in life, there is a flip side to the coin: focus can also be the very reason for things not going well for many people. When your focus is directed towards something unwanted, it can feel all-consuming and have consequences that may not be so favourable.

Activating your RAS on purpose is all about changing the things you are consciously aware of and to do that, we need to go a little deeper first.

Which brings us to the unconscious mind!

Your Unconscious Mind

The definition of 'unconscious' according to *Oxford Languages* is *"not awake and aware of and responding to one's environment"* or *"done or existing without one realising"*. The unconscious is simply everything outside your immediate awareness. Whilst the first definition could relate to being physically unconscious, there's a metaphor in that too: when we become aware of this part of the mind, we start noticing possibilities we couldn't see before - the ones that were right in front of us all along. That's the moment we activate our RAS.

Your unconscious mind, which is located in the right hemisphere of the brain, is the powerhouse that drives you, your thoughts, feelings and behaviours. It's where all the information happening outside of you is received and processed, even the bits you're not consciously aware of. It's the machinery running in the background - the part of you that makes decisions, forms judgments and reacts long before you consciously think about it.

The great thing about the unconscious mind is that it runs on autopilot; it takes care of countless processes without you having to think about them. It ticks along doing its job!

The jobs it has are really important and there are a number of them to do. I'm going to take you through just a few of them so you can begin to grasp how they contribute to the creation of your reality.

I feel for you

Let's talk emotions – the good, the bad and the ugly! Your emotions are not something you pick and choose as you go through your day; they just happen and most people have little control over them. James consciously knew that the way he felt and how he was behaving made no rational sense. This is because emotions happen automatically – they are an unconscious process. Arguing them away with critical thinking and analysis of why you shouldn't feel them doesn't work. You can give yourself a break when your feelings don't seem logical... they're not meant to be!

You are responsive by nature and whilst you can consciously choose how you want to feel and may use many of the fantastic techniques to help you do that (such as embodying and imagining the feeling you desire, affirmations, breathing deeply and smiling), when you go about your day, you feel the wide variety of emotions that are available to us as humans. Everything, from happiness, sadness and anger to guilt, fear and every other emotion in between and the feelings you experience happen unconsciously in response to internal and external factors.

It's all in the bag

All of your memories – the positive and the negative, every single one that has ever happened to you – are stored in your unconscious mind, even those things you can't remember consciously, no matter how hard you try. If you were to try to remember what a particular person said to you at your seventh birthday party just before you opened your presents, that may not be so easy to do, yet even though you can't remember it, the memory is stored away in your unconscious mind. This is the reason why you may find yourself randomly remembering things, events and conversations that took place years ago that you'd completely forgotten about. The memory was always there; it was just tucked away in your unconscious until that moment.

If you've had the privilege of being on this planet for some years, the chances are you have more than a couple of memories stored away from different times in your life. From childhood to leaving school, starting your first job, maybe getting married, having a family and beyond. For you to mentally make sense of all those memories and distinguish the difference between something that happened five years ago, 10 years ago, yesterday, today, or even something you imagine happening in the future, your memories are organised within your mental timeline – an internal filing system that is totally unique to you. Your unconscious filing system is where all the files of your life are recorded, stored and ordered in a sequence, so you can differentiate the time at which they took place.

It's important to note that not all memories are created equal and this is where your unconscious mind is extremely clever! There are those memories that, when you think about them, bring you complete joy. Then there are those you might prefer to forget about entirely.

Some memories will have a lot of emotion attached to them and at the time those emotional events occurred, you may not have been in the position to deal with them, mentally, emotionally or even physically. Here's where the clever part comes in. Your unconscious mind takes those memories and puts them in a metaphorical box, hidden out of sight with a lid on it. This allows you to go about your everyday life without having to think about and deal with any memories that are too painful in that moment. Your unconscious mind's job is to protect you and so it will keep those memories repressed until you are in a position to be able to deal with them.

The very nature of life means that you will inevitably have experiences you could call 'character building'. Events that result in you becoming stronger and more resourceful; what doesn't kill you makes you stronger, right?!

When you deal with and overcome hard times, you build mental and emotional strength and you're then in a position where you feel equipped to handle those things in the future, things you wouldn't have been able to in the past. We've all had an experience that, at the time, felt impossible to overcome, but now you would find it much easier.

Your unconscious mind has all of your memories logged and stored away for a later date, ready for when you can deal with them. It recognises when the strength needed to work through them is available, when you have the internal resources to cope. It's only then that those repressed memories will be presented to your conscious mind; you will become aware of them so that you can finally resolve them and let go of any associated negative emotions.

The time those memories are presented is, more often than not, when things are going great and you find yourself thinking about something from the past, a time in your life or an event that wasn't as good. Although it may seem to appear completely out of the blue, it is because you are ready for it – you can deal with it! Your unconscious mind will only ever give you as much as you can handle, so see this as a good sign that you must have grown. It's an opportunity to learn from the past, let it go and move forward even stronger.

Like most things in life, the first time we do anything, it can feel impossible, from playing an instrument, lifting weights in the gym, asking someone out or talking in public, to name a few. When you do it, your mind proves that you're okay and you can handle it; you build mental resilience. The more resilient you are, the more your mind will give you to work through. This offers a whole new perspective: what could be seen as something negative can be reframed as something really positive.

Just relax. I've got it

You may never have given this much thought before now, but your body is so clever; it just does its thing and works, hence why you don't have to think about it. You can rest easy knowing that, unless there is a problem, your heart will just keep on pumping and you will keep breathing every single second of the day.

69

How wonderful that your body runs itself. You have your unconscious mind to thank for that! It takes care of the running of your body for you, so you don't have to think about it. In fact, one of its most important functions is to run and preserve your body.

Your unconscious mind also knows what health is and how it feels when the body is running exactly as it should. This is why you know when you're feeling unwell – even if you're not sure exactly what is wrong, you know that something is. You have the blueprint of perfect health stored within you and when it's not present, there will be a signal that tells you so. This could come in the form of a niggle that something isn't quite right or that you need to slow down. Maybe something feels off and the voice in your head keeps prodding you to listen. We've all experienced those times when we chose to ignore the subtle signs until they got bigger and louder and we discovered that we were right! The number of times I've told myself I need some rest and I kept going anyway – that is, until my body made me rest. Whether it's through illness or injury, eventually your body will give in. Those signs, signals and whispers are your unconscious mind, so practise listening to them and trust yourself rather than waiting to prove yourself right.

Your wish is my command

There is one role of the unconscious mind that I know you are just going to love. Unlike many people, it relishes being told what to do. Finally, you have someone you can just give instructions to and they will be welcomed with open arms. Hooray! And the best news is that someone is you.

But like anything in life, instructions can sometimes be misunderstood, so there are a couple of keys to make sure the instructions you give yourself are received by your unconscious mind in the way you intend.

The first key is that the instructions need to be super simple and very clear. Sounds obvious, yet it can easily become anything but straightforward.

Being complicated doesn't mean something is better. It doesn't necessarily add depth or intelligence; it can just complicate things and your unconscious mind does not respond well to confusion. The best way to really get to grips with this is to think of your unconscious mind as though it is a young child, so make your instructions as easy to follow as possible.

Imagine you're in the supermarket with a young child and you ask them to get some tomatoes. That's a pretty simple instruction to follow, but it's not a very clear one. There are so many varieties of tomatoes to choose from, everything from fresh tomatoes, including cherry, plum, salad and beef, not to mention the tinned options of chopped, plum, with added herbs... A young child is likely not to know where to begin and so will most likely pick the one they see first. You may well be hoping for one type of tomato and end up with something completely different to what you actually wanted. This lack of clarity is true in all areas of life, not just when buying tomatoes. Consistency is also key, because a lack of it confuses the messages we give our unconscious mind.

The messages we give out are often mixed. Imagine that one day you told a young child that they are great, that they can do anything they put their mind to and they should go for their dreams. Then, the next day, you told them they are worthless and should stay at home and hide under a pillow before someone sees them and realises how rubbish they are. I dare say you wouldn't dream of it! Yet that is exactly how so many people treat their unconscious mind, which is ultimately how they are treating themselves. Having an aspiration or dream they are excited about, but then telling themselves not to go for it because they're not capable of achieving it. Feeling good one day and then beating themselves up the next. Taking steps towards something and then completely backing off again.

The unconscious mind takes on all instructions and even if they contradict each other, it will follow them all. This is not only confusing to you but also to others outside of you. It appears to the outside world as being flaky and inconsistent, like someone who is constantly changing their mind, feeling up and down and never sticking to something or seeing it through. This is something I used to do every hour, never mind every day and I imagine you have experienced this in yourself at one time or another in your life.

Always give very clear and consistent instructions to your unconscious mind, even if you don't quite believe them to be true yet. Just like a young child learning to ride a bike, the more you do this, the easier it will become. Be kind to yourself like you would be to a young child, too. If you find yourself being anything less than compassionate, stop and consider if you would ever treat another person, let alone a child, in the same way. You were a young child once and whilst you have grown up, that child still exists within you. The kinder you are to yourself, the more love you will have available for others.

The next key to making sure your instructions are received correctly is to ensure they are focused on what you want rather than what you don't want.

This is really important. It's super simple when you know it and although it's such a common mistake, it can be easily rectified. The reason this is critical to creating your reality is that the unconscious mind doesn't process negatives. I'm not talking about whether you're trying to be positive or not; this is referring to words that negate: words such as don't (do not), won't (will not), can't (cannot). The negating word doesn't register with the unconscious mind, so when you instruct yourself NOT to do something, all your unconscious mind will hear is the instruction itself.

Let me demonstrate how this works. If I asked you to NOT think of a red apple, I can guarantee you would think of a red apple. This is because your unconscious mind processes what to think about in order to NOT think about it and your attention is then on that very thing.

This happens a lot when people are pursuing goals. Many people find it easy to tell you exactly what they don't want and spend their time and energy in an effort to avoid those very things. Affirming over and over again about how...

"I don't want to be in debt" – the focus is on debt and how much you have

"I don't want to mess up this pitch" – focus is on the pitch going badly

"I'm going to stop eating chocolate" – all you can think about is chocolate

"I'm going to make sure I don't miss my target" – your attention is now on missing it

"I'm not going to hit the snooze when my alarm goes off" – snooze, snooze, snooze

"I'm not putting up with a toxic relationship" – you find toxicity in every partner you meet

"I won't be in the job I hate by this time next year" – oh no!

The list goes on!

If you're constantly telling yourself what not to do, that is the message your unconscious mind will process. It will be the movie that plays in your mind, the things you think about and focus on. Aside from the fact that it will hinder your progress in achieving your outcomes, it's not the best movie to watch over and over again. You'd never choose to watch a film that kept repeating a scene you didn't want to see, a movie that doesn't feel good, yet this is how people live their lives.

You are literally giving your mind instructions all day, every day, through the things you choose to focus on. So, always focus on and say what it is you do want rather than what you don't want.

If you don't know what you want right now, that's okay. The starting point to knowing what you want is to know what you don't want, so you're already on your way! You can begin flipping the direction of your thoughts by considering what the opposite of the unwanted things are as you continue working your way through this book.

When the instructions you give your unconscious mind are clear, simple and focused on the outcome you desire, you activate your RAS to find ways to fulfil those instructions. It is on high alert whenever an opportunity that matches it is within reach.

It's all about me

This is a really interesting one. If you've ever found yourself saying anything less than nice things about someone or something, then this is very important to know: your unconscious mind takes everything personally. It doesn't know that your thoughts or words are being directed at someone outside of you and so it takes it as an instruction or suggestion to itself. It's very literal! This is where the saying *"when you point one finger, three fingers are pointing back at you"* comes from. If I were to give you any advice, it would be to say nice things about others and really mean it. This may take a little practice when you first begin, but when you truly know that you really can be, do and have whatever you want in your own life, it makes sense to wish everyone else well in theirs, too.

If you ever find yourself experiencing any negative emotions about the success of others, it's okay. We've all been there! Watching someone else having the very experience or achieving the thing that you want but haven't yet can certainly bring those emotions to the surface. The truth is that those emotions have absolutely nothing to do with the person or thing that prompted their appearance. It's really about you and the beliefs about lack and scarcity that you hold about it being possible in your life. That lack could be in the form of a belief you hold that limits or emotions that prevent you from also achieving it.

Think about it like this. If someone across the road bought themselves a new fancy lawnmower, the way you feel about that neighbour and their lawnmower is nothing to do with them. If you wholeheartedly believe that you, too, can have a lawnmower, or you don't really care about lawnmowers at all, then you'll probably feel nothing about their lawnmower either. You may not even realise they have one! Whereas, if you didn't believe you could have the same lawnmower, maybe you couldn't afford it in that moment, or you didn't think you'd be capable of using it, then you may well have negative feelings about the neighbour and their lawnmower.

Usually, people will direct the lack they feel towards their neighbour, calling them names like 'show-off', 'shallow', 'all about the money', 'compensating for lack in other areas' – all without cause or any factual evidence to support such accusations.

When those emotions come out to say hello, it's a powerful opportunity to turn them back onto yourself and ask, What is really going on? The lawnmower itself, or any other garden machinery, object or occurrence in life, is irrelevant; it's purely a representation of you and what's going on internally. How you perceive others is actually extremely useful information about you and what you believe to be possible. It's the best feedback we could ever wish for! Rather than pointing the finger at others and noticing what you don't like about them, consider for a moment why that might be. What is it within you that needs addressing that is being reflected at you?

It's also worth keeping in mind that your own unconscious mind will take any negative thoughts directed at someone else personally as a suggestion to yourself, which will programme your own mind to think that way. Asking for something you desire and then resenting the presence of it will only push it away further. If you believe that people who are successful in something you desire must be untrustworthy, unethical, dishonest, or unkind, then unless you see yourself as sharing those traits, you'll unconsciously block yourself from achieving similar success. You may resist becoming successful because of who you believe you'd have to become to get there. Remember, that's just a belief and there will always be examples that prove it isn't true. Your response to the world and others is the window into your unconscious mind.

This concept works both ways, so there is the opposite side too. Any time you notice the good things outside of you, those things are also true about you. For you to notice them in others, they must be within you in the first place. Recognising them is an opportunity to reinforce what your inner being already knows. Even if there are some things you aren't fully on board with being true just yet, just accepting that it's possible on some level is a step in the right direction.

If you have been anything less than positive about others up to now, which we all have at some point, give yourself a break. Everyone is doing the best they can with what is available to them in that moment. Hindsight is a wonderful thing and it's easy to look back at how you would do things differently given the same experiences. Let's face it, if you hadn't had those times where you may have behaved in a way that makes you shudder when you think of them today, then you wouldn't have had the opportunity to learn from them and be who you are now. The power you have to change things is always now!

Willpower wears off

Willpower. Even the word itself feels like hard work and if you've ever tried making changes through willpower alone, then you'll know that it is! Willpower often requires going against ingrained habits, thoughts and behaviours.

The problem with that is the habits and behaviours we have are not what we consciously choose; they are formed in the unconscious part of our minds. No matter how many times you tell yourself you will stop biting your nails or heading straight to the fridge the minute you walk through the kitchen door, your unconscious autopilot kicks in. It's usually only after the event that you realise you've done it. Even if you consciously manage to intervene in the moment and stop yourself, it's not easy to do and uses a lot of energy to resist, because those programmes run automatically. Your mind is continuing to think about or do the thing you don't want, even if your body isn't. So even though the chocolate may have been left in the cupboard, your mind is there with it!

To relate this to the rowing boat and the submarine, imagine the rowing boat (your conscious mind) has been heading in a particular direction for a while, to a destination called Frustration Town. I'm sure you can guess by the name that it's a frustrating place to be!

The rowing boat is floating along every day, sailing closer towards a destination that you don't really want to go to. Frustration Town is where you're pushing hard but never quite breaking through. You second-guess your progress, question your timing and wonder why, despite everything you're doing, it still doesn't feel like enough. It's where your results don't match your effort and it can feel like you're failing, but you may not be sure why it's happening. Although you don't want to go there, the actions you take continue to lead you in that direction.

Being the ambitious high achiever that you are, you decide to make changes. You feel determined and motivated and so you take action to do just that. You begin turning the boat around.

You use your oars to point yourself towards a new destination, a place called Success Town, where life is, you've guessed it, you are living a life that you deem to be successful. It's a place of aligned achievement. You're performing at a high level, but it feels lighter, more intentional. You have clarity and you're accomplishing your goals in a way that feels good.

The changes needed to get there are happening. You're taking action, doing the work and surrounding yourself with people who have already mastered the winning formula. You are metaphorically pushing your oars hard from inside the rowing boat, making a conscious effort, thinking about your choices and putting in the effort to succeed. Bit by bit, you begin heading towards your new destination.

It sounds good, right? But there is an issue!

You're pushing really hard, tirelessly working from inside the rowing boat, but what you haven't considered is that the rowing boat is still tied to the submarine and the submarine hasn't been reprogrammed. It's still set to head towards Frustration Town and so it carries on its usual route. No matter how forcefully you row, you're fighting against the big submarine under the water, pulling you in the opposite direction. Determination will only keep you going for a while and it soon becomes really tiring. The submarine is just too big and eventually, the pull from it feels so strong that you run out of steam and stop fighting it.

When you think about making changes in this way, it's no wonder so many people give up when willpower is the only thing that got them started in the first place.

Our unconscious programmes make carrying out patterns of behaviours easy to do with very little cognitive effort, which is super helpful; it means you don't have to think about every little thing you do day to day. You are programmed to brush your teeth, drive a car and cross your arms, all without thinking. (Try crossing your arms the opposite way to what you usually would and notice how much you have to consciously think about where they go!) Imagine having to think about absolutely everything you do. There wouldn't be time for anything else but the basics, if you even made it that far!

These programmes are also amazing when they are pro-grammed to take you towards your goals. They are not so helpful when they are programmed in the opposite direction. This leads to so many people giving up when they don't see the instant reward for the effort they put in. Change through willpower and conscious effort is flipping tough and, because it takes a lot of brain power, when results don't happen quickly or easily, it feels too hard to carry on. Giving up becomes very appealing and people will reason with themselves as to why it's a good idea to do so.

I spent many days telling myself that life is short and it's important to enjoy it, so I should have that extra dessert or glass of wine; I shouldn't wear myself out working too hard, getting up early every day – I could die tomorrow! Whilst you could say this is all true, it's really looking for excuses to not make progress, because it feels too much like work, like a battle and no one wants to go to war, especially with themselves. Your conscious mind looks for the logic behind giving up, but the problem is that your unconscious mind knows the truth. It knows your desires; there may just be a mismatch between what you want and the beliefs and drive to support you in getting there.

All of that being said, willpower can win out over a period of time, although it's less common, as most give up before reaching the threshold needed to make it stick. There are varying studies that show it takes at least 21–66 consistent days to form a new habit using conscious willpower alone. The 21-day theory was first discovered when Dr Maxwell Maltz, a plastic surgeon in the 1950s, performed operations. He noticed a trend of people taking 21 days to adapt to new situations in their lives. This included everything from having a nose reconstruction to a limb being amputated. After 21 days, he found that people had adjusted to the change. New research from Phillippa Lally has since found that the average time it takes to perform a new behaviour on autopilot is 66 days. Either way, the message here is that continuous repetition is key.

When you make changes consciously, the rowing boat is attempting to pull the submarine along with it. Bit by bit, day by day, slowing the submarine down until it can be redirected. This absolutely can be done and just like a rowing boat pulling a submarine, it's not easy. When you consciously tell yourself you are going to do something and your unconscious mind, your thoughts, beliefs, self-talk and emotions don't match what you are saying, it feels as tough as pulling a submarine in the opposite direction of the path it's programmed to follow.

The unconscious mind has been programmed to head in a specific direction and it becomes familiar with the route; it's known, it feels safe and so it's easy to revert to the comfortable, most trodden pathway, even if it's not the pathway that leads to where you want to go.

Changes through willpower can be done and one of the biggest keys to making them stick is consistency. To change the submarine's direction, it needs to be pulled a little bit, every single day for 21–66 days in a row. Consistently really does mean consistently!

When you begin your new way of being, if at any point during the 21–66 consistent days you happen to slip up and revert to old behaviours and habits, the submarine returns to its original track, heading back towards Frustration Town. Carrying out the unwanted behaviours before the submarine has fully reprogrammed its route will cause the submarine to resume its path. If that happens, the 21–66 days reset and you have to begin again from Day One, pulling the submarine a small bit at a time!

To put this into a real-life context, if someone gives up smoking and doesn't have a cigarette for 15 days in a row, the submarine will begin to slow down, ready to re-route itself in the direction of being a non-smoker. The habits are starting to form and become the new way of thinking and behaving. If, on Day 16, that person has a cigarette, the submarine reverts to the original unwanted path. It resumes the thought patterns, beliefs and drivers that support them in being a smoker and so they feel compelled to behave like one, i.e. to smoke. The submarine is back on its original route; it just took a slight detour for a while.

There is something positive that happens in the process; all is not lost!

By this point, the submarine has spent some time pointing towards and treading the new path, even if just for a short period of time, so it has a reference point for the new route and there was a little momentum created on the way. This makes it much easier to go that way again because the mental muscle that shows you that it can be done is already in place, which makes picking up those metaphorical weights easier to do a second time around.

If you do manage to keep on track consistently for 21–66 days, having practised the new way of doing things without reverting to old habits, the submarine is then reprogrammed to head for the desired destination, to Success Town. It gets to the point where it's easier to keep going, to continue carrying out the new way of being, than it is to go back to the original route. It becomes the new automatic programme and, most importantly, the rowing boat and the submarine are going to the same place, cheering each other on. This is alignment!

Consciously pursuing something you haven't done before, whether it's learning a new skill or behaving differently, will usually start with you being completely unaware of how to do it, or it may feel unnatural to you. This is really hard mental work; there can be a lot of frustration and confusion and giving up can seem like the easier option. But if you keep going, one day at a time, there comes a point where it suddenly seems to slot into place and you can just do it – it happens easily without thought.

To help make changes you are more likely to stick to, choose to focus your attention on completing just one day at a time. Doing so takes it from what can feel like a mammoth task to just accomplishing something for 16 hours, since you'll probably be asleep for the other eight. At the end of every 24 hours, you will feel like you have achieved a mini goal, which will spur you on to do more. It will then feel less about willpower and more about carrying on with the good work you have already done.

I remember when I decided to start learning to play the guitar, I kept forgetting to even practice. I had to put it on my phone calendar with an alert to remind me; otherwise, I unconsciously carried out my usual activities and it was only at the end of the day that I remembered I'd forgotten.

The first time I picked up a guitar, I felt like I was holding an alien and it sounded like it was out of tune. After a few months of consistently practising (thanks to my alert reminding me to), even though it was hard and my hands physically ached at times, I could suddenly play a few chords without having to think about what I was doing and it sounded like a real song! Picking up my guitar in the evening became something I just did without thinking. This same principle applies to change across the board.

The point at which things begin flowing is when the programming in your submarine has changed – you're on track and the route to Success Town is now the default direction. That doesn't mean there is no more effort required on your part; it's just that the effort no longer feels like your mind is in opposition and using any energy you have to fight it. Your energy can then be utilised to do the work necessary to achieve what you want. Amazing!

Having a purpose, a reason for making the change, is such a huge motivator, too. If there is no reason for doing it, then even the most disciplined would struggle to carry on. We'll talk more about this in later chapters.

Now, I should mention here something that can happen after your unconscious mind has been reprogrammed. It's totally normal for your conscious mind to question things. Being the critical thinker that it is, you may find yourself analysing those changes to convince yourself that it's actually happened. For such a long time, the submarine has been heading towards Frustration Town… and then it's not and that can be a little disconcerting. It may take a little time for your conscious mind, sitting in the rowing boat, to be certain that the change has happened, that the submarine has really altered its course. If you find yourself feeling sceptical, you now know why and you can just let your conscious mind catch up and be convinced the change has taken place in its own time.

Programming itself is neither good nor bad; it's both wonderful and not so wonderful at the same time. Carrying out the majority of what we do without any brain power allows us to focus on the things that matter to us and require our energy at that time. We are able to carry out the daily tasks without any thought. The first time you learnt how to tie your shoelaces, it probably felt like an impossible task that you would never achieve, until one day you did. You kept practising and eventually your unconscious mind took over. The programme for how to tie your shoelaces became automatic – you can now do it without consciously thinking about it and this is true of many of the things we do. Programming is hugely beneficial in our lives. This programming also means that much of what we do without thought, even when it isn't serving us, is completely out of our awareness. We just do it and even if we know it's not what we want, it feels easier.

Many of the things we want to stop or start doing, we know about, but not always. So often, the things we do that sabotage our success are entirely outside of our awareness – we are oblivious to them because we do them on autopilot. Bringing those unconscious patterns into conscious awareness is the first step in changing them. You have to know what it is that needs changing for you to be able to do it.

Activation Tool – Uncovering Unconscious Patterns

At the end of each day, note down the following:

- **What habits, behaviours and thoughts did I carry out that aren't serving me?**

- **What did I do that is keeping me on the path I no longer want to be on?**
- **What did I do that stopped me from heading towards my goals?**
- **What didn't I do that would help me move towards my goals?**
- **What can I do instead?**

Once you have identified the patterns you're running that are no longer serving you, there are ways you can make changes very quickly at the unconscious level, which will turn the submarine towards Success Town. If a habit or behaviour is created in the unconscious mind, then it makes sense that changing it also takes place in the unconscious mind. Where it's created is also where it is re-created into something new.

Understanding how lasting change is created is a crucial part of knowing how to make it. You can then begin piecing together the picture of you in relation to what's materialising in your life. The world that you see outside of you, what you are conscious of, all begins and is based on the reality that you hold in your unconscious mind, as within, so without. NLP is the user manual for your mind and the gateway to creating quick and lasting change.

4

Training Your Mental Filters

The important things will always make themselves known.

What is reality? Well, if you were to ask five different people, you would get five different answers, which really makes the point that reality is what you perceive it to be in the moment that you observe it. It's an ever-changing thing and no two people in the entire world ever have, or ever will, experience reality in the exact same way.

Reality is everything that is happening in your awareness at any point in time. Wherever you place your focus in any moment is the only thing that is actually happening in your world right then. Remember, most of the things surrounding you, you won't even notice; your conscious mind just won't process them. You are oblivious to them until you focus on them. Does that mean they weren't there before you fixed your attention on them? Of course they were!

Everything that is happening outside of you, all that you are experiencing, every second of every day, is being taken in through your five senses: what you can see, hear, feel, smell, taste. When I say everything, I mean *everything*! Studies in NLP show that we receive approximately 11 million bits of information per second. To give you an idea of just how much that is, imagine 11 million jellybeans or 11 million people in a stadium bombarding your senses every second of every day. Even if you like jellybeans, that's a lot to process. It's jellybean overload!

It's probably no surprise that your brain isn't able to deal with that amount of information at the rate it's coming in, not consciously anyway. Think about it. If you had 11 million jellybeans coming at you in one go, how could you possibly take in all of the different sizes, the different colours, the tastes, the smells, the sheer number of them? The same thing goes for real life: how could you be aware of every detail that is happening outside of you? The simple answer is, you can't. And the truth is, you probably wouldn't want to be. The amount of information your conscious mind can focus on and handle at any one time is limited. It's not physically possible to consciously process 11 million bits at any one time. As a result, there are a massive number of events happening that are completely beyond your awareness.

The fact that most of what is going on around us all day, every day is outside of our awareness is a good thing; otherwise, we'd have a meltdown – our minds would go into overdrive. It would be like opening up every programme on your computer all at once: there would be too much to handle and it would crash!

You can rest easy knowing that even if your reality isn't how you want it to be yet, your mind is keeping you sane; it's protecting you. It's one of the reasons you have two minds!

There are many practices that help you change your focus and therefore your experience of reality and the real question is, what influences our focus and our perception of reality in the first place? What determines which of the 11 million jellybeans or bits of information made their way through the conscious mind and which bits stayed unconscious? When you can get to grips with that and have an understanding of how to change it, you open up your mind to possibilities that had previously gone unnoticed.

It's time to welcome back your reticular activating system! The gatekeeper to your reality. We're going to dive into the mechanics of how your RAS is linked to what information is getting in and what is staying out.

The Mental Security Guard

Your name's not down; you're not coming in!

Imagine, for a moment, a gatekeeper stood outside a building, with a list of what can come in and what cannot and the rule is that if it's not on the list, then it's not getting through the gate!

This is how your RAS works. It's the gatekeeper of your mind, filtering out anything that isn't on the list and only the things that are will be let through the door. It's only the things on the list, the ones that do get inside, that you then become aware of – they have been allowed into your conscious mind. The rest stay outside the door in your unconscious mind. All of those things left outside are still there. They still exist; you are just oblivious to them.

This begs the question: how does something make its way onto the list?

Years ago, I would take the same route to work every day of the week. I knew the journey like the back of my hand and paid very little attention to my surroundings because I'd seen them hundreds of times before. Then, one day, I was chatting with my mum, who is a Reiki master, amongst other things and loves her crystals. She told me she had been reading about a particular crystal that had all sorts of healing properties and she really wanted one. Being a big believer in energy, she wasn't keen on ordering it online, as you never quite know what you'll end up with or be sure about the quality of the crystal, so she was keen to find one that was ethically sourced and genuine.

It was around November time; Christmas was approaching and I had yet to buy presents. In fact, I hadn't even thought about what to get everyone, so I was pleased she had made it easy for me. The crystal was added to my Christmas gift list.

A day or so later, I was doing my usual drive to work when I noticed a shop tucked in between an insurance office and a nail bar. I had never seen this little shop before, so I assumed it must be new. I looked in the window and saw it sold hundreds of different crystals. When I arrived at work, I jumped online to have a look at the shop and to my surprise, it turned out it had been there for years. I had to question myself. I'd driven past it hundreds of times and never spotted it. How was that possible?

How had I never noticed it? Why did I suddenly catch sight of it on that particular day, shortly after I had been speaking about crystals? The shop had always been there, or at least as long as I had been driving past it.

The crystal shop is just one example of the many things I drove past every day without even realising they were there. Everything from bike stands, lampposts and the flowers in the window above the shop next door to the droopy curtains in the flat opposite, your unconscious mind is taking in every single bit. Remember, we are processing 11 million bits per second, so if you were to compare that to even the latest smartphone with an impressive memory capacity, taking in the same amount of information as we do, it would be full in no time at all. We manage to go through our entire lives with a constant stream of data to deal with and so our mind helps us out to make sure we don't go crazy!

To be able to handle all the external information that is consistently inundating our senses, we have a set of internal filters. These filters very kindly help you to literally filter through all of that data based on what is and what is not on the list!

The List Filter

Many years ago, a friend of mine was getting married and boy, did she have the wedding of the year planned. The more planning she did, the more the wedding seemed to grow. The guest list got bigger each week until the point she wasn't even sure who half the people on it were. It became unmanageable. It was too much for her to take in and so her mind started to filter itself down. She started to forget some of the people she'd invited. When guests had forgotten to specify their meal preference on their RSVP, she thought they weren't coming to the wedding. With so many different groups of people from different sides of the family and different friend groups, she had merged them all into one another. Her experience of the wedding and the people attending was so different from what was actually happening because of how she had filtered the experience.

Your mind uses its magical mind filters in three different ways to whittle things down. These filters are designed to make your life easy, to take away the gigantic overload of the outside world and make it manageable. They do this through a process of deletion, distortion and generalisation. This is taken from the NLP model of communication, which explains how we filter our external world.

Let's go into the three different filters and how they each work, so you have a better understanding of the gatekeeper's criteria for what makes it onto the list.

Deletion

Most of the information coming in through your senses is completely deleted from your awareness, in that you don't even register it. You quite literally don't see things that are right in front of your eyes because your filters have deleted them from your world because they are not important to you in that moment. To make it simple to understand, let me give you an example of deletion in action, a scenario that you've probably experienced in some form or another yourself...

Three people enter the same room for a course on making the perfect pizza dough. After leaving the training room, they are all given a questionnaire to complete. One of the questions within the questionnaire is not about the training content or the course itself; it's about things that were around them in the room.

The question is, how many plants were there in the training room?

Person One answers: *"There were plants? I thought this was about food! I can't say I noticed any. I'm going to have to say none."*

Person Two answers: *"Two or three, I think? Maybe more, I'm not too sure."*

Person Three answers: *"There was a peace lily, a fiddle-leaf fig, two aloe vera plants and a pink orchid."*

All three people were in the same room at the same time, yet they all answered the question very differently. Here is where it gets interesting, because at least one of the plants was directly in their eyeline, but their own internal filters will have determined whether or not they were aware of the plants. If plants are important to a person, they will have been brought into their conscious awareness. The RAS will have sent a signal to the brain to say, *"Look over here. There's a plant."* If plants are not important, then they may well have looked directly at the plant and still not consciously registered it. The gatekeeper will have determined that this 'plant' isn't on the list and so it's not getting in!

Whilst this is an isolated story that probably has very little impact in the grand scheme of things, think about it in terms of the whole of life. How many opportunities, people and experiences that could help you to achieve success, are you completely oblivious to because they've been deleted from your experience?

What are you not aware of that, if you were, would be the answer to the question you may not have asked yet?

Distortion

If you've ever been given something that was intended to be a compliment but you took as an insult, then you'll have an idea of how distortion works. When you mistake something for something it is not, your perception of reality has been distorted.

I remember as a child being absolutely certain that every time I heard a floorboard creak, there was a burglar in the house! Whilst this wasn't true, in my reality, in that moment, it was and my body would respond to it. My heart would race. I imagined someone sneaking around the house wearing a balaclava and I felt scared. I was experiencing it as though it were real.

I had taken the sound of the creaky floorboard and distorted it into something completely different. This doesn't just apply to children with highly active imaginations; it's something that happens to all of us every second of the day. Someone could be genuinely offering you help or guidance, but through your filters, you interpret it as them showing off and so you dismiss it. There could be an opportunity staring you in the face that will propel your goals forward and you view it as a scam, looking for the catch – it's too good to be true. Disclaimer here: that doesn't mean there aren't scams out there; it does mean there could be times where what is being offered to you is being met with resistance because of a distorted perception of it.

If you were to look at things through a different lens, what else could they be?

Generalisation

One of the ways that you handle all of the information coming in is to unconsciously categorise it into groups, to make it more manageable. For example, each time you see a moving vehicle, you don't have to think about whether it's a car, motorbike, bus, lorry, etc. You know these are all examples of vehicles and therefore, they move and take people from one place to another. If you didn't generalise information, then every time you saw a moving vehicle, you would have to think about what was in front of you. Just imagine, for a moment, if you weren't able to categorise 'cars' as being 'cars' and every time you saw a different make, model, colour, engine size and so on, you had to consciously think about it as being something completely new... there would be little room to do anything else. Thank goodness you can generalise information!

Generalisations are also the basis of beliefs. Let me give you an example of this: take a child who passes their spelling test and is then told by their parents and teachers that they are so clever and good at tests. Bravo! That child could take what they have been told and believe it is true and so a belief has been formed that they are clever and good at tests.

Years later, when they may be taking a whole range of different tests, they apply this belief to everything they do. They generalise the information across many other areas of their life. Whether it's a driving test, a piano exam, or something they deem a person needs to be clever for, like learning a new language, they have generalised the belief that they can do anything. Pretty useful!

Of course, like anything, there is a flip side and many people generalise events and create beliefs that aren't empowering either. Another child may fail a test and then apply it to not being clever enough at everything they do, concluding that they are a failure. Whether good or bad, wanted or unwanted, generalisations are powerful at influencing our perception of reality as we know it.

Time to bring this together and give you an idea of what's going on outside of you versus how you are experiencing it from the inside. Continuing with the theory of NLP, from the 11 million bits of information that your unconscious mind is taking in every second of the day, you filter it down to make it manageable for your conscious mind to process through deleting, distorting and generalising. Now, here's the bit that's worth paying attention to... From those 11 million bits, you whittle it down and are left with a much smaller amount and that smaller amount is the part you are aware of; that information is what your conscious mind notices. Here's the crazy part: from those 11 million bits per second, you are only left with and aware of approximately 126 bits of information every second.

WOAH... How much?

Imagine you're in a stadium with 11 million seats, all filled with people. In any second, you would only know that 126 of those people sat in their seats exist. Your unconscious mind is taking in the other 10,999,874, but the gatekeeper isn't letting them in. Their names aren't on the list and so they are staying outside.

Apply this to your life for a moment and think about how many opportunities are happening right in front of you every second of the day that you aren't aware of. The answers to all of your questions are ready and available for you. All you have to do is change what you let in and what stays out.

Which begs the question, how does your brain choose which 126 bits it will let through the gate?

The 126 bits you are left with, the information you perceive in your world, is filtered through your unconscious mind, where your beliefs, values, personality type, memories, concepts about the world, your attitude and everything that makes up you and your version of reality. This is the reason why your unconscious mind holds so much power – as mentioned in Chapter 3, 95% of what you do happens without you even thinking about it; 95% of the thoughts you have, the things you say to yourself, the behaviours you carry out, the way you feel, all happen on autopilot. When you make changes to the programming that runs the unconscious mind, the filters are adjusted and the things you delete, distort and generalise in your experience will be different. The world outside you is like a projector reflecting back to you the world inside of you. When you change your thinking, you change your focus.

Acclaimed author and screenwriter James Redfield said, "Where attention goes, energy flows." Attention is your focus and it's the very thing that activates your RAS.

Here's an overview of how your focus and attention work in relation to your RAS. There are three different factors your RAS is activated by and search for.

· **The things you deem important. These are influenced by your deepest motivators, preferences and beliefs and are stored in your unconscious mind. They are the programs you are running in your metaphorical submarine.**

· **Your name. Sounds simple, yet this is why you can be in a crowded room of people and still hear your name mentioned in a conversation that's taking place a few feet away from you.**

· **Whether or not your partner wants sex. Really? It's true! That piece of information filters its way through all of the other noise, so no matter what else is going on around you, you just know when they are feeling frisky!**

Your RAS is doing you a massive favour. It's lightening the load and doing all the heavy lifting for you. Just think how much energy and mind power it would take if you had to sit with your list and filter through everything. It would be exhausting to the point that you would get nothing else done.

Your job is to use your conscious mind to train your RAS in knowing what weights to lift. You want to direct its focus to spot the very things you are looking for and keep out all the distractions that are in opposition to it. When you master that, the life you desire is reflected back at you in all its glory.

If you don't like what you see, or you want something different, you need to begin changing your attention and focus.

Let's bring back the red car for a moment.

As soon as your attention is aimed towards a particular thing, your RAS is activated whenever that thing is present, hence the reason why when you decide you want a certain car, or anything else for that matter, you see it everywhere. It's not a coincidence; it's the science of your brain!

Follow along with the brief exercise below to experience how the RAS works in a very simplified way.

- **Look around the room and notice everything blue.**

- **Then close your eyes and try to recall everything red –**

difficult, right?

- **Keeping your eyes closed, say the word 'red' to yourself at least 10 times – visualise the colour red vividly.**

- **Then, open your eyes again and notice how your attention is drawn to everything red – you start seeing green everywhere that you didn't notice before.**

The colours in the room were always the same, yet because of your focus, your RAS jumped into action and was activated to look for a particular thing: the colour red. Your perception is filtered by intention. If you're always looking for problems, you'll find them. If you start looking for solutions, you'll find those too.

The best way to decide what the gatekeeper lets in is to create the list you want. Be the boss of your own RAS.

Time to get focused!

5

Attention = Acceleration

Intention plants the seed for what is to come.

Intention is a powerful thing; it directs your focus and energy. When you set an intention, there is an energetic charge behind it that is more powerful than wishing, hoping or dreaming. It has the potential to move things in the direction you want, activating your RAS to home in on and consciously bring what you are seeking to your awareness.

"Seek and you shall find"

Matthew 7:7

This quote states that if you actively look for something, you will find it.

To give you a little science behind why intention is so powerful, I'm going to give you a very brief overview of quantum physics and how it affects our external world. This isn't something I'm an expert in, so bear with me here...

We live in a world of energy, which consists of waves and particles. Waves transport energy from one place to another. They're not localised and they are not something you can point at or hold in your hand. They move and create patterns, much like the wave of ripples that form in water when you throw a stone in. Particles, on the other hand, are solid matter – what we see, hear and experience in our reality. They are localised and so you can point at them. They move linearly.

Those waves of energy consist of an energetic field of possibility. All possibilities that could take place exist in a waveform and at any moment in time, there are multiple choices and multiple realities that we have the opportunity to experience.

Everything that could exist, does exist!

The thing that turns those waves of possibility into a particle – in other words, what turns the possibility of something being real into reality itself – is our observation of it. When we observe something, we bring it into our existence.

From all of those waves and all the possibilities they bring, there is the wave that is most likely to materialise. This is known as the wave of probability, the most probable version of reality that you will experience. Listen up because this is where intention comes in.

Your intention directly impacts your focus and it is your

focus on a particular thing that takes it from being a wave of possibility and turns it into physical matter, your reality. The observation of the wave turns it into a particle (the physical matter stuff you can touch). The act of consciously observing it takes the wave of potentiality and collapses it into a particle. Observing something or focusing on it actualises it in your world.

If this has piqued your interest, I encourage you to do your own research to discover more. There are many experiments that have been carried out over the years, including the famous double-slit experiment by Thomas Young in 1802. I recommend popping 'double-slit experiment' in your search engine if you're keen to find out more.

Whatever you decide to do, your intention will direct your focus and that focus increases the likelihood of it happening. It takes all of those possible experiences and whittles them down to the most probable. The most probable being the one that has the most energy flowing towards it.

Here's a simple way to understand intention in this context. Imagine you are on a boat and in that boat, there are 50 cabins. You are informed that 25 of the cabins are run-down with no luxuries, just the necessities to accommodate you.

The other 25 cabins are quite the opposite. They have been upgraded to give you an experience fit for royalty.

However, you don't know which cabin is which. Your only job is to choose which cabin door you will go through.

This is where intention becomes really important. There are multiple waves of possibility, in other words, multiple paths you can choose from and your intention and focus influence which one you move toward. Of all of the waves of possibility, all the cabins available, the one that you actually open the door to will be influenced by your intention.

That doesn't mean that having the intention of choosing a cabin of luxury guarantees that you will. It also doesn't mean that it won't, but it does mean that you can intend to have the experience you desire regardless. If you were to decide that you'll only be happy if you choose a cabin of luxury, then the experience you have is out of your hands, as you're no longer in control of how you feel. The response is dictated by external events.

Think back to the universal Law of Cause and Effect: living a life at the mercy of whatever is thrown your way, placing any responsibility for your life outside of you, which leaves you powerless to do anything about it.

If you intend on having a great time and being the one who is responsible for this, regardless of what cabin you end up in, you will have a very different experience from relying on the cabin to deliver. Your intention will influence the experience you have of whichever cabin you choose.

Setting an intention to have an amazing time will activate your RAS to notice all the amazing possibilities wherever you end up and you will filter your reality accordingly. Your RAS is on high alert to bring to your attention the very things that you have decided are important and so you are focused on.

If you intend to have a wonderful time and you happen to open the door to the run-down cabin, your RAS will find all the ways it is wonderful. You may then see the room as a place of solitude, without distraction, or somewhere you can relax and enjoy simplicity and being away from the busyness of the world.

When you base your experience on whatever happens around you, you may not even end up enjoying or even noticing the luxuries when you do open the door to them.

Always make sure you set your intention in a way that directs your focus towards the experience you want to have.

Asking Better Questions

A simple way to change the direction of your focus and improve your life is to ask better questions. The questions you ask automatically train your RAS to look for matching evidence

Think of your RAS like your very own internet search engine. The questions you ask are the answers you will find. I spent years asking myself versions of the same question: 'Why me?' or 'Why can't I...?' and my RAS delivered evidence to match. So many things came from a place of lack, scarcity and a belief that nothing would change.

Asking myself those questions provided me with the answers to them. I continually found evidence that supported the reasons why I would never be a success, make money, have a happy relationship, or feel as good as other girls. The more evidence I gathered, the more I believed it to be true. My RAS continually brought to my attention everything I was focused on. The problem back then was my intention. Whilst it's not my proudest moment, on some level, I wanted those things to be true. If I could prove to myself and others that I didn't have what it takes, that it wasn't my fault, it was the cards I was dealt and the universe kept showing me that what I was saying was true, then my fate was out of my hands and I didn't have to take responsibility for my life. I was so scared that if I took a leap of faith, I would fail and so I kept myself safe by playing small. If I didn't go for anything, then I couldn't get it wrong.

The problem with this is that it didn't stop me wanting those things. After years of kidding myself and pretending that life was better without the risk of messing up, I had a realisation. I was actually a Jedi Master of creating my world. I'd become so good at finding the answers to the questions I was asking myself that it was almost scary. I would only have to ask myself, why was I so rubbish at everything I did? Why could I never succeed at anything? What did I have to offer in a relationship? And often that same day, the evidence would come flying at me. I would have job applications rejected, or my partner would cheat on me and actually tell me the person he cheated with was much prettier, had more money or was better in some kind of way. I looked for the answers and I found them. It dawned on me that if I could do that, then surely I could create the things I actually wanted. I thought that I was rubbish at focusing, when the opposite was actually true. I had just gotten so good at focusing on what I didn't want my life to be.

I'd love to say that having that realisation changed everything overnight, but the truth is that, like anything in life, it takes practice. An easy place to start is by changing the questions you ask yourself. Make it your intention to ask better questions and find better answers.

Turn the 'why can't I/haven't I/don't I?' questions into a 'how can I?' question. That question alone will dramatically increase the possibility of a solution coming your way. Asking *why* questions can encourage rationalisations for why you find yourself in a certain position. That's the conscious mind kicking in as a protection mechanism. Asking *how*, *where*, *who* and *what* questions will activate your RAS to run those questions through its filters and put your mind on high alert whenever an answer is present. It will look for all the ways, *how*, *where*, *who* and *what* for you.

How can I...?

Where can I find...?

Who can help with...?

What can I do about...?

This can also be used when you notice yourself making statements that are limiting you from achieving what you want.

"I can't do it", "I'll never have...", "I don't know how to..."

Instead, turn them into a question of

"How can I do it?"

"How can I have...?"

"How can I learn to...?"

"What do I have?"

One Thought at a Time

When you change your thoughts, you change your life and there are some thoughts that you have probably been thinking for what feels like FOREVER! The thoughts that are deeply embedded and ingrained into your unconscious, the ones that feel like they are stuck for good and no amount of positive thinking will shift.

Well, if you were hoping to be excused at this point, to see yourself as the exception, then I'm sorry to be the one to disappoint you. Those deeply embedded thoughts hold no more power than new thoughts and beliefs you created a week ago. The only difference is that you have been thinking them for much longer and so the connections in your mind are well rehearsed.

Because of this, when a new thought comes along that contradicts it, the old way of thinking has the advantage of power in its corner. Labelling these long-term thoughts and beliefs as being more significant reinforces them and gives them power. There will be thoughts that have a much bigger impact on your life than others, but either way, they are just thoughts and thoughts can be changed.

It's the world of paradox - a thought is nothing more than a thought; it's not real and yet thinking something makes it real, so therefore it is the most powerful thing.

Think of your thoughts like footprints in the snow. The ones you have been thinking about for some time have created a pathway that you walk along often and so the ground is well trodden. This is the same in your mind. When you keep thinking thoughts, the connections in your brain keep firing over and over again, which makes it easier for them to do it each time. Your unconscious mind's primary role is to keep you safe and so it likes the familiar and it always looks for the easiest route for you to get where you are going. Even though the thoughts you keep thinking may not be serving you, they are known, so they feel comfortable. They also take minimal effort, because you have already thought them so many times before and so your mind will go to those thoughts first, as they are the path of least resistance, the easy route.

The first time you think a new thought, it's like creating a new pathway in the snow. There is no obvious route; the steps will usually feel a little harder to begin with and there may be more effort required as you haven't walked that way before. Walking in thick, untrodden snow can be hard work. The easier option is the one where you keep walking on the path that is worn in, but if that way of thinking isn't getting you what you want in life, then is it really the easiest option, or does it actually make life harder?

A life of regret is hard; a life of feeling unfulfilled is hard; a life you don't enjoy waking up to is hard. When you look at it like that, thinking new thoughts is absolutely the better option and something you can do.

When you keep walking the new path consistently and focusing on thinking new thoughts, eventually that becomes the path most trodden and the old path, the old way of thinking, is filled with snow and it's no longer the easiest route to walk; those old thoughts are no longer the easiest to think. The new embedded thoughts become your new default and so you start thinking them automatically.

Doing this process consciously will take a little time and practice, but one thing that's for sure is that the time will pass anyway. You're always going to have thoughts, so you might as well start changing those unwanted ones. Whilst the concept of creating your reality is often focused on the physical outcome you'll achieve as a result, the real reason to do any of this stuff is that it feels good! Thinking negative thoughts feels rubbish, so it makes complete sense to begin to change them. If you're reading this book, the chances are you have a desire to make positive changes and achieve big things. I guess that the reason you want that is because of the way you think you will feel when it arrives. Waiting for something outside of you to change how you feel inside is being at the effect of it. It's using the reasoning that the result will cause you to feel good, which puts responsibility for your feelings outside of you. If, instead, you set an intention to experience what you want and then concentrate on feeling good regardless of the outcome, you put yourself in the driving seat – you become the cause of the effects in your life. You are the creator! When your focus is on that, the wave of potential is more likely to turn into the wave of probability through your observation of it.

Easy to say, right? But where do you begin when the thoughts you currently have are miles apart from the thoughts you want to have? The simplest way to begin changing them so you start to feel good right now, while simultaneously working towards your goals, is by taking it one thought at a time!

Without the small things, the big things would not exist; never underestimate their importance and power.

Jumping from an unwanted, ingrained thought to a new, wanted one that is so far removed and feels completely out of reach tends not to work so well. The gap is too big and the current thought fights to stay put, reaffirming its truth.

If you've spent years, maybe a whole lifetime, telling yourself you're not worthy or you'll never be rich, then thinking *I am worthy, I am rich,* is just too much of a leap. Even if it isn't serving you, your mind wants to protect you and that thought or belief is what it knows, and so it feels safe.

We all have to start from wherever we are right now, so rather than beating yourself up for not being where you think you should be, fighting the thought or pushing against it, instead accept that it's just where you are, not where you're going and be kind to yourself. Resisting it is placing your attention and focus on it – and so it persists.

Take one step at a time!

To begin changing an unwanted thought that is far from your new desired thought, you need to bridge the gap. You do this by creating stepping-stones to the new way of thinking by reaching for something slightly more towards the thought you want and something you can believe, taking you in the direction of the new thought a little bit at a time.

Changing a thought, even just a little, has a compound effect on everything you do and it's something that anyone can do immediately. The key, then, is consistency!

Activation Tool – Bridging The Gap

In the previous Activation Tool, Uncovering Unconscious Patterns, you made a note of the thoughts that aren't serving you and what you want instead.

Using the list you created, identify which ones seem far out of reach and carry out the following steps.

- **Create three columns as below - Fill in the unwanted current thought and the desired thought column using your list.**

Here are some examples:

Current Thought	Bridge	Desired Thought
I'll never be as naturally talented as others		I'm talented and my mindset and preparation give me the edge
I don't have what it takes to win		I have what it takes to win
I always have bad luck		Good luck always find me

- **Bridge the gap.**

Create a bridge to take you from the current to the desired thought. This should be a stepping-stone rather than a jump towards the new thought.

The step must be one that you can get on board with. It may not be something you are thinking yet, but it must be a thought that you think is believable. If the step is slightly smaller than you would like to begin with, that's okay – it's still a step in the right direction.

Here are some examples:

Current Thought	Bridge	Desired Thought
I'll never be as naturally talented as others	Talent helps - and I'm improving every day through intentional training and focus	I'm talented and my mindset and preparation give me the edge
I don't have what it takes to win	I'm learning what it takes to win and I'm getting closer every time I show up	I have what it takes to win
I always have bad luck	Sometimes things don't go my way, but I'm learning to spot and create more opportunities	Good luck always find me

· **Practice the new thought.**

Once you have your stepping-stones in place, it's time to put them into practice, one thought at a time.

Another really simple way to bridge the gap is through the use of time and process.

Process: Rather than the current thought being a finite position, it turns it into something that is moving and changing towards the new, desired thought.

For example, I am in the process of gaining the edge, so I have what it takes to win.

My luck is in the process of changing.

One powerful and simple way to shift limiting beliefs is by using the concepts of **time** and **process**. It helps to soften rigid thoughts and open the mind to possibilities.

- **Time: Add "yet"**

Adding the word *"yet"* to the end of a limiting belief implies that change is possible – it's simply a matter of time. This small shift rewires the brain to expect growth rather than assume failure.

Example:
"I don't have what it takes to win."
*"I don't have what it takes to win **yet**."*

This creates space for potential and progress, rather than shutting the door.

- **Process: Frame it as a journey**

Instead of seeing a belief or current thought as a finite position, it turns it into something that is moving and changing towards the new, desired thought.

Example:

"I'm in the process of gaining the edge I need to win."

"My mindset is shifting – I'm starting to see more opportunities."

"My luck is in the process of changing."

This reframes it as something that is in motion and evolving. You're able to bypass the resistance to affirmations that feel untrue. Instead, it gives you a believable, empowering narrative that respects where you are and then aims you towards where you're going.

Catching yourself in the moment may sound easier than it is because most of what we do is unconscious; we're not even aware of some of our thoughts.

Really begin to pay attention to your thoughts and how you are feeling. If you're feeling bad, then I can guarantee you're thinking a negative, unwanted thought.

Every time you become aware of it, in that very moment, start by saying to yourself, either in your head or out loud if possible,

"That's okay."

You are interrupting the thought, letting your unconscious mind know that it's safe and giving yourself a break all in one go. Then, take a deep breath and say to yourself,

"I've got this and I know [insert the new thought]."

You're reassuring yourself. And the truth is, you have got this. I believe in you!

If that thought feels too far out of reach, again, it's okay. It's all feedback and you can just create a stepping-stone before that one that is slightly less of a jump.

Remember, the important part is that it's something you can get on board with.

· **Affirm the new thought.**

Time to take the new thought to the next level!

Set an alarm or a reminder on your phone every hour, two hours, three hours... as often as you can (but no longer than four).

When the alarm goes off, check in with how you are feeling and take a moment to honour that feeling. Congratulate yourself for taking the time to acknowledge and become conscious of your thoughts.

Take a second to remind yourself of the new thought, the stepping-stone. Think about that thought and imagine how life is when that new thought is true. Notice what you see, hear, feel and know.

Once you have that feeling, turn up the dial, increase the better-feeling thought to twice the intensity, then three times the intensity. Focus on it and really indulge in it.

· Set your intention

Next, set an intention for the hours between now and your next alarm.

Set the intention to continue to focus your thoughts on the stepping-stone and in the direction of your desired thought.

· Repeat

When the next alarm goes off, take a minute to notice how diffcrent you felt over the previous hours. Be aware of the things that you have perceived in a new light and how your thinking is beginning to change, even if only for a minute here or there... It's still progress!

It will take repetition to create those new thought connections in your mind. Each time you think the new thought, you are walking in those new footprints in the snow, so it may take some work and practice to remind yourself to do it.

Pat yourself on the back for taking the time to do this exercise. This is the work of changing your reality from the inside out. Imagine how differently you will feel a year from now when you do this every day!

Remember to always ask yourself *how* you can instead of *why* you can't!

6

Turning Vision into Measurable Results

"The day you plant the seed is not the day you eat the fruit."
  Fabienne Fredrickson

You've set your intention; you know what you want; you've visualised it, strategised around it, taken steps towards it, so where is it?

After months of picturing my new red car on the driveway – imagining my hands on the steering wheel, planning the trips I'd take and feeling the satisfaction of owning it – I still didn't have the car.

One of the most famous teachings in the manifestation world is the phrase *"ask and it is given."* It was popularised by Esther Hicks in the Abraham-Hicks work and the idea is simple: when you ask, the universe responds instantly. In other words, the moment you form a desire, the energetic blueprint of it exists. The challenge isn't in the asking – it's in becoming a match for what you've asked for.

At the time, though, I didn't fully understand that. To me, "ask and it is given" sounded like a promise of speed and certainty: decide you want it and it's yours. But rationally, I knew I wasn't going to open my eyes and find a car sitting in the drive with the keys in the letterbox. I accepted, on some level, that the things I wanted existed as possibilities already – but if it was "done," why hadn't I received it?

I spent hours analysing how it could happen, trying to work out the exact route to success. Maybe I'd win one in a competition. Maybe a long-lost relative would leave me one. Maybe someone close to me would have a windfall and surprise me with a gift. My imagination kept circling improbable options and instead of feeling inspired, I felt stuck, discouraged and disempowered. I wanted the results immediately, but my belief in that happening didn't match my desire.

Later, I came to understand something essential: turning an idea into physical reality involves a time delay. Asking, whether out loud or internally, is just the spark – the first moment of creation. What happens after that spark isn't instant or dramatic; it's the gradual process of things organising themselves in the background as you continue to take consistent steps forward. What matters is what you do in the space between the spark and the result. Just as in sport, business, or any pursuit, results don't arrive instantly. They compound over time through consistent focus, energy and aligned action.

Realising this was a relief. I wasn't failing, I wasn't "blocked." I had simply misunderstood the process. The car hadn't fallen from the sky and landed on my driveway because that's not how creation works. There's always a lag involved in turning thoughts into physical results – a process we are all participants in.

When I first heard this, I felt such comfort in knowing I wasn't going mad; I wasn't broken. I was finally able to give myself a break when material goods didn't appear within an hour of deciding I wanted them. That understanding shifted everything. The delay isn't a punishment; it's a natural part of creation. And far from being frustrating, it can actually be one of the most exciting parts, because it's in that space that you grow into the person capable of holding the result.

Of course, if you're a driven go-getter, that delay can also feel like the most infuriating part... you want everything yesterday! But once you accept that the waiting period is where alignment, growth and readiness are built, you start to see it differently. The space between asking and receiving is not wasted time. It's the training ground for the life you're creating.

I didn't see it that way. I was impatient and focused on what I didn't have. And neuroscience shows us that the brain filters evidence to match your dominant focus. By fixating on lack, I was literally programming myself to see more lack.

Once you see the time delay as part of the process and space for growth, everything shifts. You can start treating your attention like training time, your emotions are the fuel and your consistency is like the reps in the gym. Joe Dispenza puts it perfectly: "Where you place your attention is where you place your energy." When you understand that, you realise you're not waiting for the universe to deliver – you're conditioning yourself to receive. You are the one responsible for and therefore in control of, how quickly things change.

The timescales involved in physical creation vary from person to person based on many factors, including their starting point, their reality as they currently experience it and their ability to see past it. However, I'm going to share with you some guidelines and the factors that speed up or slow down the lag between deciding what you want, taking action and actualising it. To explain the process of thoughts becoming things, the timescales to physical fruition and how to get there, we're going to continue a little more into the world of the quantum field. Hold on tight!

Energy of Creation

Earlier on, we touched on how the world we live in is made up of waves and particles. We essentially live in two different worlds that are linked and interact with each other: the quantum and the physical.

The quantum world is the energetic space of possibility. Every thought, every feeling, every spark of imagination you have lives here first. The physical world, on the other hand, is the dense world of particles - the tangible "stuff" we interact with through our senses: what we see, hear, touch, smell and taste – the things we can measure.

Everything that exists in the physical world was once energy. Nothing in our physical world would exist without the thought, the idea, or the possibility.

That might sound a little abstract, but think about it. Every car, every company, every invention started in someone's imagination before it became something you could drive, buy, or hold in your hand. The thought preceded the form. This is a physical creation that can easily be reverse-engineered, but creation is not limited to the cars that exist; the principle is true for all manifestations.

Now, extend that principle to your own life. Every relation-ship, every opportunity, every milestone you've ever reached started with a thought. Whether you realised it at the time or not, you were creating.

Going back to the universal Law of Cause and Effect: for every effect, every creation, there will have been something that caused it. The question is, are you creating on purpose or is life happening on autopilot?

Two Worlds

In the quantum world, possibility is instant - there's no time involved. This is where the phrase 'ask and it is given' comes from - the idea that the moment you project a desire, it already exists energetically. The wave of possibility has been set in motion. The process that turns the thought wave into physical matter is the observation of, or focusing on, it.

But here in the physical world, there's a delay. Waves don't instantly appear as solid particles. Energy needs focus, repetition and time to condense into matter.

This is where most people get stuck. They ask, they visualise, they feel good for a moment... and then, when nothing drops on their doorstep by morning, they call it quits. They think the process isn't working when in reality it's already underway.

Let me put it in performance terms; think of going to the gym. After your first workout, you don't expect to walk out with abs, but you also don't think that nothing happened. You trust the process because you know your body is already adapting, repairing and strengthening beneath the surface. With each rep, each set, each day of showing up, you're stacking momentum.

Manifestation works the same way. The moment you ask, the adaptation begins; you just might not see it yet.

You have probably heard the question of whether or not a tree that falls in the woods makes a sound when no one is around. Using this model, the answer would be no, because unless someone observes it happening, it doesn't exist in their reality. Sounds are an interpretation of vibration and to interpret something, it has to come through at least one of our five senses. The very act of observing and measuring something is what turns a wave of potential into a particle.

Frequency, Vibration and Focus

Every thought and emotion you hold creates a wave. That wave has a frequency - how fast it cycles. Each cycle consists of an up and down where the wave reaches its peak (the highest point) and trough (the lowest point). The wavelength is measured by the completion of a cycle, which is the distance between the peak of one wave and the peak of the next and the distance between the trough of one wave and the trough of the next.

Think of it like a wave in the ocean hitting its crest before it comes back down again, falling below the surface of the ocean where it hits the lowest point, before working its way back up again (see Image 1).

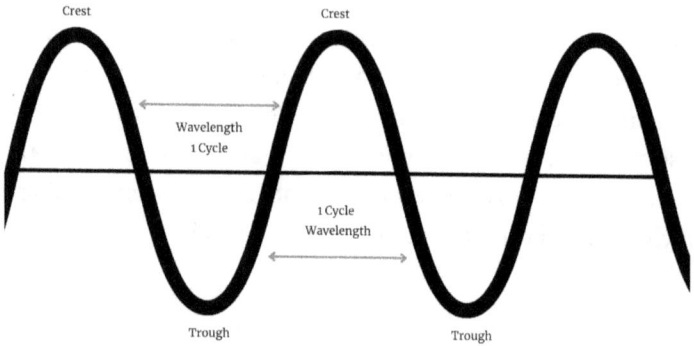

Image 1

Your thoughts and feelings emit a wave and each wave vibrates at a certain frequency. Frequency quite simply refers to how often something happens or, in this case, how frequently the wave completes a full cycle.

To recap from the universal Law of Vibration, higher-frequency waves have more cycles per second; lower-frequency waves have fewer cycles per second. The lower the frequency, the denser and more solid things appear. Particles are very low-frequency waves vibrating at such a slow rate that they appear as solid matter.

Everything is energy; everything vibrates! It's the Law of Vibration.

Everything includes you; it includes all of us. For every thought we think and the way we feel about those thoughts, we are emitting a wave that has its own frequency. High-frequency feelings are those such as peace, joy and love and they feel light in their energy; the frequency or the rate at which they vibrate is faster. They have a high number of wave cycles per second, so each wave cycle follows the next very closely.

Low-frequency feelings such as grief, guilt, sadness and despair all feel heavy in their energy; the frequency at which they vibrate is much slower. They have a lower number of wave cycles per second; the waves are longer, they have a bigger gap between each of them; they don't follow as closely together. They feel denser; there is a gravitational pull and so the weight of them can be felt.

You can feel the difference. Walk into a room with someone who is "high vibe," and their energy lifts you. Spend too long with someone radiating stress and negativity and it will drag you down.

Good-feeling high-frequency waves vibrate at a faster rate than not-so-good-feeling low-frequency waves. There is more energy and momentum behind them and so things happen more quickly, which brings us to how this relates to the time it takes to create physical manifestations!

This model is based on many studies I have come across, including the work of Joe Dispenza and Gregg Braden, who are true experts in their field. I've modelled the graph below on Peter Sage's talk 'The Art of Living in Through Me'. It shows a visual representation of waves and the frequency at which they vibrate, demonstrating the link between the frequency in relation to the timescales involved between thoughts and things.

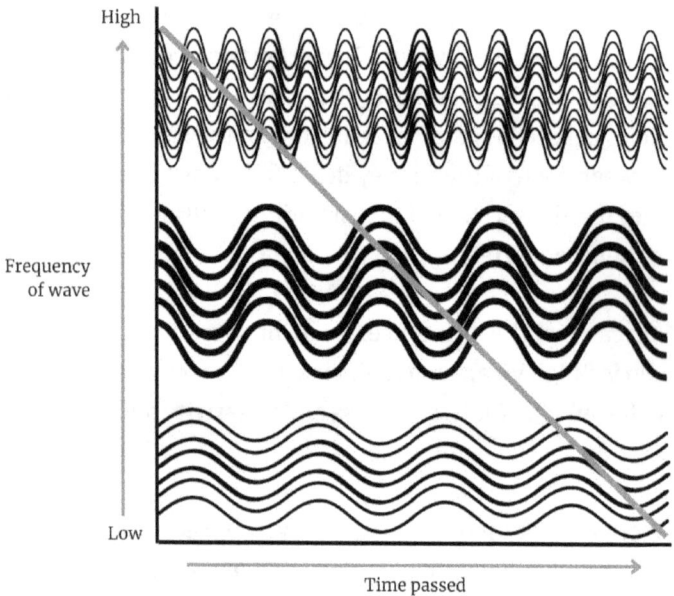

High

Frequency
of wave

Low

Time passed

On the vertical axis, you'll see the frequency rate of the wave, starting with a low frequency at the bottom of the axis and a high frequency at the top.

The higher the frequency, the more frequently a full wave cycle is completed. This results in there being more wave cycles per second. The lower the frequency, the less frequently a full wave cycle is completed and so there are fewer wave cycles per second. The higher frequencies have a smaller gap between wave cycles than the lower frequencies.

On the horizontal axis, there is a representation of the time it takes for a wave to transform into a particle, or a thought to turn into a thing.

When a person is vibrating at a low frequency, when they feel those low vibrational emotions, there are fewer wave cycles per second and therefore a bigger gap between each wave. The fewer the number of cycles per second, the longer it takes to create physical results. When a person is vibrating at a higher frequency, when they feel those high-vibration emotions, there are more wave cycles per second and so there is less of a gap between each wave and so the time to physical creation is less.

Now, here's why this matters for performance:

- High-frequency emotions build momentum. They close the gap between intention and result.
- Low-frequency emotions slow the process. They create drag, resistance and delay.

This doesn't mean you'll never dip low - of course you will, you're human. But the more time you can spend resonating at

133

higher frequencies, the faster the tipping point arrives.

The Tipping Point

Everything builds toward a tipping point: that magical moment when energy turns into matter. It's the point where your unseen focus suddenly produces visible results. The Quantum to Newtonian transition point.

The tricky part is that you don't know when that tipping point is coming. It's like pushing a flywheel - it feels heavy at first, hard to move, but eventually the momentum builds and suddenly it spins with far less effort.

This is why sustained focus is non-negotiable. A quick burst of positivity is like one workout... great for a mood boost, but it doesn't rewire your reality. It's the consistent reps, the sustained attention, that change your baseline.

The tipping point doesn't just deliver "the thing" you asked for, it provides evidence - small shifts, signs, opportunities that tell you you're on track.

Sustained focus and energy are generated from the unconscious mind - the default setting that is always running in the background, even when your conscious attention is elsewhere.

Back then, I thought creation was about the event. I'd sit down for 10 - 30 minutes, meditate, visualise and get into the feeling of already having what I wanted. During those moments, it felt incredible. I was in a state of flow, I was aligned and the frequency I was broadcasting was high. The number of cycles per second I was emitting energetically was rapid and coherent, which is exactly what speeds up the creation process.

The problem was, I didn't sustain it. Those higher frequencies only lasted as long as I was sitting in the chair. Once I stepped back into daily life, my unconscious programming took over. An argument with my partner, a bill arriving, a traffic jam and within minutes, my frequency dropped back down to my old default. The gains from those 30 minutes were drowned out by the other 23 hours of the day.

What I didn't realise at the time was that the unconscious mind is always the one running the show. You can create short bursts of focus consciously, but unless your unconscious patterns are being trained to hold that higher frequency, you'll slip back into old ways of thinking and feeling. It's like rowing hard in one direction while a powerful current drags you back the other way. The current is your unconscious mind and unless you work with it, it wins.

If I'd continued to broadcast at that higher frequency consistently - if I'd sustained it beyond those short daily bursts - the results would have eventually become evident in my physical reality. This is the piece most people miss. They think of manifestation as a ritual: a few minutes of visioning, then back to "normal life", but normal life is where the real creation happens.

It's what you sustain that counts. Just like one intense workout won't transform your body, one great visualisation won't transform your reality. The change happens in what you do, think and feel the other 23 hours of the day. If most of that time is spent unconsciously broadcasting low-frequency thoughts of lack, frustration, or worry, then that's what you're rehearsing, reinforcing and creating.

This is why change comes down to training. The conscious mind can spark an intention –the unconscious mind sustains it. When your unconscious patterns are aligned with what you want, the "default" becomes supportive rather than sabotaging.

Think of it like athletic training. A single high-intensity session spikes your heart rate, but it doesn't change your resting heart rate. What creates lasting adaptation is repetition, doing it often enough that your baseline shifts. In the same way, it's not about how high your frequency is during meditation - it's about raising your everyday baseline so your unconscious mind naturally sustains it. Sustained practice comes from how you carry yourself moment by moment.

If any of this relates, I invite you to give yourself a break because we are all doing the best we can at any moment in time. Knowing what you know now, you would likely do things differently, but without those experiences, you wouldn't know what you do today. In a few years, you'll probably look back at the things you're doing now and wonder, *What was I thinking?* I certainly plan on that being the case because that is the beauty of growth and hindsight. If you find yourself wishing you'd done things differently in the past and being unkind to yourself for the choices you made, see it as the blessing it truly is. You have learnt from the past and the future will be better because of it.

During that period, there were times when I'd pull myself up on my negative thinking and make an effort to consciously think more positively. Still, the problem was that the minute I wasn't consciously holding myself accountable and paying attention to my thoughts, my unconscious patterns kicked in and I snapped straight back to my default setting. When I stopped trying to row the boat in a different direction, pushing hard on the oars, using conscious effort, the submarine, my unconscious mind, carried out the automatic way of thinking, feeling and behaving and so I reverted back to my default ways of doing things. The day-to-day frequency I felt back then was pretty low most of the time, with only the occasional high. I wasn't particularly aware of how bad it felt because I didn't have a lot of experience to compare it to. Life seemed like a slog and because it had gone on for so long, it felt normal. Getting through the week was the name of the game!

To relate this to my own experience of how focus shapes outcomes, the frequency I sustained for the majority of the time was low. Those higher-frequency moments were few and far between in comparison, which is a really important part of the puzzle.

Think of it this way. If someone spends an hour a day focused on their goals, but the other 23 hours thinking in the opposite direction, the energy and overall emotional balance are still tipped in favour of and directed towards the unwanted. The key is what's sustained, not what's momentary, because it's sustained energy that creates results and 23 hours a day is pretty sustained. This is also true of spending a week totally focused on what is wanted and then turning the focus to wondering where the physical evidence is. The energy hasn't been sustained for a long enough period and the switch in focus slows down or pauses any momentum that was in play.

Now, this doesn't mean you have to spend 24 hours a day completely and utterly focused at all times on exactly what you want, although if you do that, then you are demonstrating intentional leadership of your life and kudos to you!

Whilst 24 hours of all your attention and focus in one direction is not realistic because we're people living a physical experience, things happen and our focus turns to the unwanted. We feel rubbish. You can absolutely adjust your internal filters so that, for the most part, you see the world through the lens you desire. For everything we desire, its opposite must exist – the other end of the scale. These moments of distraction actually offer contrast and clarity. We are constantly being shown where our limitations are through our internal response to the external world. The key is to take the feedback and switch your focus. The more you practice this, the quicker you will become at it.

If you were to spend just 51% of your time focusing your energy on the things you want to create and the other 49% focused on lack, then the scales would tip. They would have to. Spending 51% of your day feeling good and placing your attention on the great things you already have and the excitement of knowing what is coming would be a massive shift for most people. This is easier than it first sounds because around six to nine hours each day will actually be spent sleeping, so you only have to focus on things turning out how you want them to for about nine hours a day. Let me rephrase that: you have the privilege of and can enjoy spending at least nine hours focusing on life going as you desire and feeling great just because you can.

Energy is power that can be transformed from one form to another, from waves into particles. In the context of creating your reality, energy is all about your feelings and the power and force behind them. The more intense and good feeling the emotion is, the more energy is present. This is something we have all experienced at some point in our lives. You can set an alarm to wake you up at 3am to catch a flight for your holiday and bounce right out of bed. When that same alarm goes off at 6am to go to a job you dread, suddenly that energy has disappeared; it's curled up in a ball under the quilt. In both scenarios, you're waking up, yet the energy behind it is different and the reason it's different is that one feels great and the other maybe not so much.

Focused energy is placing your attention on the feelings that you believe the physical creation of your desires will give you – being able to generate the energy in advance of creating and receiving what you want, which is really the reason for wanting it in the first place. Feeling good shouldn't be something that feels like a chore and if it does, it may be a sign that your methods are rooted in escaping your current reality rather than moving toward what genuinely lights you up

I've mentioned before that the timescales of change can vary. What's important to understand is that transformation at the energetic level—where ideas and intentions begin- often mirrors transformation in the physical world. In both cases, results take time to become visible.

You wouldn't go to the gym, do one intense workout, then rush home, stand in front of the mirror and panic because your muscles hadn't suddenly appeared. Even though you can't see the changes instantly, you trust that your body is already responding and adapting.

Yet when it comes to creating new results in life, so many people lose faith the moment they don't see instant evidence. They forget that the same principle applies... just because the results aren't visible right away doesn't mean nothing is happening. Energy shifts first, then matter follows.

It's accepted in the physical world that our results correspond with our input. In other words, the effects we see in our life are a direct consequence of the thoughts, behaviours and actions that came before them - the Law of Cause and Effect in action.

Take training as an example. If someone consistently worked out four times a week for a period of weeks, the evidence would become visible. The exact results would depend not only on what they did in the gym, but also on what they did outside of it - nutrition, rest, hydration, recovery. All of these factors combine to accelerate or slow down progress.

It's the same in every other area of performance. Just because the outcomes you're working toward aren't visible imme-diately doesn't mean nothing is happening. Like muscle growth, change is often invisible at first, but it's always in motion and the things you do outside the "spotlight moments" matter just as much as the high-intensity efforts. Writing the proposal, making the call, refining your mindset, managing your environment, how you carry yourself day to day - it all compounds.

In the end, you don't become what you occasionally do. You become what you consistently do. Sustained focus is what builds momentum and the more you sustain it, the faster the tipping point arrives where progress becomes visible and undeniable.

Think of how you spend your time focusing like watering a plant. If you have two plants, one that is the wanted plant and one that is the unwanted plant, which plant grows? The answer is the one that you feed. If you continue to feed the unwanted plant, then it will stay strong.

Your sustained focus is the water. If you focus on feeding the wanted plant, that will be the one that gets stronger and the unwanted will be starved in the process. Over time, the unwanted plant will shrink, making it even harder to focus on.

Choose the plant you feed wisely!

Of course, like anything in life, it takes practice. No matter where you are, you will find yourself going backwards and forwards with your focus. It's called being human. The

141

more you practice, the easier it gets and your baseline default frequency rises and you become more attuned to the higher good-feeling vibrations. Those feelings then become the very thing you want to experience more of, regardless of the physical evidence that follows, which becomes a by-product.

One of the common hold-ups that people have in this process is wanting instant results, which is understandable. If you're anything like me, when you know what you want, you want it yesterday. A great way to overcome this is to find ways to enjoy the progress rather than the outcome.

This, of course, can be easier said than done, so let's relate it to going on holiday to bring to life why it's so important and how it can be fun. The journey begins by deciding you want to go away – your outcome. This is followed by looking at destinations, hotels, the activities you will do whilst there, the food, the culture and anything that may be on your list of important criteria. Whilst you're doing this, you're not actually on your holiday, but you have started the process of getting there and it's usually an enjoyable one. Once you've decided exactly where you're going, there is potentially some shopping to do – new beachwear, sandals and sun cream to buy. You're still not on your holiday, but it's definitely fun. Then comes the packing... There will always be parts that are less enjoyable than others! I know people who relish this task and like any steps to creation, there will be things you have to do that you savour less than others. A great question to ask yourself when those tasks arrive is, How can I make this fun? Put your favourite music on, dance around whilst you do it, turn it into a party... whatever works. Then, there's going to the airport if you're flying abroad, the duty-free shopping, the flight itself, or the car or boat journey. All of these things have to happen before you arrive at your destination and whether you choose to make the most of and find pleasure in them is up to you.

Now, most people probably enjoy much of the holiday process, so here's another example. When someone begins exercising to improve their physical appearance and health and they have a goal in mind, it is also possible to enjoy the progress they make along the way to getting there. If the aim was to lose two stone, this isn't going to happen overnight, but they will lose more and more weight each week if they are consistent before reaching the two-stone mark and there will be evidence along the way that they are focused and heading in the right direction. No one would expect a two-stone weight loss instantly and it would be very concerning if that ever happened. If, due to some bizarre freak of nature, it did, the reality is that they wouldn't be ready for it; they wouldn't be prepared. They wouldn't have any clothes that fit them for starters; no one around them would recognise them; they wouldn't recognise themselves or know how their new body worked and responded to the things they are used to doing. Their new eating habits and exercise routine wouldn't have been formed to support their new body and this principle is true of all creation.

Whilst it's easy to think that we want the things we don't have right now, if they were actually given to us straightaway, we wouldn't be equipped to handle them. Even with the holiday, if you were transported to the destination right this second, I would guess several things have to happen for you to be ready for it, from shopping, packing, arranging a dog sitter, organising your work calendar, maybe you plan on having a bikini wax or haircut before you go. There might be things you need to do, things you need to change, or consequences in achieving the goal that you haven't considered, both internal and external. If you were ready for them right now, then you would have them. It's about becoming the person you need to be to have the life you want and noticing the changes happening along the way, so when you arrive, it's who you are.

Become the person you need to be to have the life you want!

Your focused energy in a single direction activates your RAS. Your RAS then searches for the things that are a match and activates whenever there is evidence that supports your achievement of it or a way to make it happen. The more you feel it, the more you reveal it, the more you notice and focus on it, the more highly attuned your RAS is. It then becomes a self-fulfilling loop of creation. If it matches your focus, your RAS will let it in; if it doesn't, you won't see it.

You are reprogramming your unconscious mind, the submarine. Your conscious mind, the rowing boat, where you sit day to day, will undoubtedly drift from time to time, focused in one moment and not the next. You may find that the waves push you backwards and forwards, but if you continue rowing in the direction of what you want, one day you may notice some land off in the distance, a sign you're heading in the right direction.

The next day, you might find something floating on the water next to you – a small box and inside it's filled with valuable items. Those items may come in the form of a person, a job, money, an opportunity, something that is taking you even closer to what you want - evidence that you're on track. Celebrate those moments, feel how great they feel and use them to focus even more on your desired outcomes. The fun really is in the journey of becoming the person you want to be.

When you ask, it is already done in the quantum world. The physical world just needs a little time to catch up. The more time you spend in a higher, good-feeling frequency, with trust that things are happening exactly as they are meant to, the quicker the results are each time. Matter is dense energy that appears solid, but it is still energy vibrating at a very slow speed and it takes time and sustained focus to turn a wave into a particle. However, that time can be as little as four to eight weeks! Any belief that things can't happen that quickly is just that: a belief. Guess what, you get to prove yourself right either way - your RAS will shine a light, leading you to the evidence that supports the outcome you believe to be true.

The wave doesn't follow the particle; it's the other way around. In other words, it's not about changing the physical world to show you proof so you trust you'll succeed and feel good about it; it's up to you to believe without seeing, feeling good and the physical world changes. It's the universal law of correspondence: as within, so without.

The most important part of all of this is tapping into the feeling of your desires being actualised. If you spend five hours a day picturing your dreams coming true, but you're not really feeling it, the energy and frequency of your thoughts will be reflective of that and so will the results you get. Our thoughts, feelings and how we show up in the world are all linked, so when one changes, the others change too. If your thoughts are truly directed towards the outcome you want, then you will feel good; the body responds to the mind and vice versa. Thinking about the thing you want but imagining yourself without it, or thinking about why you don't have it, isn't focusing on what you want; it's focusing on the lack of it, which is different and emits a different energy. You create what you focus on – in this case, the absence of your desire.

The waves of energy that transform into particles are always there and always happening. The rate at which the wave turns into matter is determined by your thoughts, feelings and how much of your time is spent focused on what you want.

Think about it... you have the potential to see massive, concrete, tangible results in your life within four to eight weeks, if not sooner. If you've already been feeling predominantly great, with little resistance to the things you desire, those timescales can be dramatically reduced. That is something to feel good about!

Activation Tool – Getting Prepared

Uncovering any potential unconscious blockages is funda-mental to being able to experience the very things you desire. Sometimes, there can be unconscious blocks that we are consciously aware of, but we pretend they are not there. Pretending something doesn't exist won't change it.

Hold in mind something you want to achieve and answer the questions below. Be totally honest with yourself.

- **What would happen if I achieved it?**
- **What would the positive consequences be?**
- **What would the negative consequences be?**
- **Who do I need to become to allow those things?**
- **What changes do I have to make to become the person I need to be?**

If you identify anything that could prevent you from achieving what you want, ask yourself how you would deal with that situation if it happened. When you know that you can deal with it, your unconscious mind will know that it's safe to allow it into your experience.

For example, when I first started running online courses, I really wanted to fill them straightaway. When it didn't happen, I was puzzled. I asked myself those very questions and uncovered that I was unconsciously stopping it from happening because, even though I wanted it, I didn't really have the capacity to handle it. There wasn't the time to fulfil everything that goes with someone new signing up and the other huge tasks already on the agenda at that time. I knew that delivering a great quality service wouldn't have been possible with the resources available and so I blocked it from happening.

Spotting this allowed me to take steps to build systems that eased the workload and then feel totally congruent and aligned with achieving the goal. The next online course filled up very quickly.

Tipping the scales

Ok, so now you've done some deeper work, it's time to have some fun because fun is a good-feeling place to be. Taking yourself and any situation too seriously in and of itself can lower the frequency of it. Being serious turns what could be a light and free feeling into something heavy. Whilst working towards the things you want, also create time every single day to do something that feels good, maybe something you can incorporate into your goals. Put it in your diary!

I've listed some suggestions below and feel free to add in your own:

Physical Recharge

- Meditate or do breathwork
- Take a cold plunge or contrast shower
- Book a deep tissue massage or facial
- Do a high-intensity workout or boxing session
- Walk, run, or bike in nature

Social & Connection

- Host a great dinner or BBQ with friends
- Attend a live sports event or concert
- Join a mastermind or social group
- Play poker, chess, or a strategy game

Creative & Playful

- Dance to your favourite song
- Listen to music and sing loudly
- Try a new adventure or experience (driving day, kayaking, hiking trip)
- Learn to play a musical instrument

Mental Recharge

- Read a great book or biography
- Watch an inspiring documentary or comedy
- Do a jigsaw puzzle, sudoku or crossword
- Write down your wins and lessons of the week

There are so many ways to feel great right now. Whilst you are on your way to creating what you want, you can certainly enjoy the ride. Feeling miserable doesn't feel good and it slows down the process. Make it your mission to learn how to feel great and practice every day.

7

Intrinsic Drive

The reason to succeed must be bigger than the reason to not.

Motivation, or the lack thereof, is one of the biggest reasons people give up, often just when things are starting to get good.

You work hard, doing all the things you think you should be doing; your foot is on the accelerator and then, for some unknown reason, you begin to put the brakes on or maybe even hit reverse, undoing all of your good work. So, it's back to square one, leaving you feeling like a failure.

I've been there many times and it can feel as though you are driving yourself crazy!

I spent so many years wondering why this was. Why did I destroy all the effort I had put in? What caused me to sabotage my own results? Why was I so motivated when I started, but as I got closer to what I wanted, the motivation wore off? It made no sense, yet it kept happening. I kept doing it.

It didn't matter if it was to do with work, career, money, relationships or my health, the pattern of destruction seemed to be consistent throughout various areas of my life. I would begin to make headway with friendships and then retreat. I would make a payment on my credit card and then spend twice as much. I'd eat healthily and look after myself all week and then go out of my way to consume as much junk food as I possibly could in the space of one sitting. It was exhausting and I wasn't getting anywhere fast!

The day I discovered what was going on and why this was happening, I could've cried with relief. First of all, I realised that I wasn't actually going mad and I finally understood one of the patterns of behaviour that I had been running. The thing with patterns of behaviour is that we tend to take them with us wherever we go. What we do in one area of life, we tend to do in all areas. The self-destruct button wasn't confined to a single problem; it spanned across many. Self-sabotage was probably the only thing that was consistent about my inconsistent motivation!

At first glance, recognising that this pattern of self-destruct ran across various parts of my life may have seemed negative, because I was sabotaging my own results in so many different ways. But simply reframing the meaning I had assigned to this changed my whole perception. If a single pattern was creating unwanted outcomes in all those different areas, then changing that pattern in just one of them — the one causing the most problems — would naturally spill over into the others. The same mechanism that had been working against me could start working for me. That was something I could get on board with!

Before getting stuck into the detail of which area of your life would have the most impact on all other areas if you changed it, let me go through the process of motivation, where it comes from and why it doesn't last.

First things first, it's important to understand that motivation is not a magical skill that some have and some don't. There isn't a pill you can take that gives you motivation, either. I remember watching people who had what I wanted and wishing I could have their motivation to go and get it. I thought it was something they were born with; they just happened to be part of a lucky group of people who were part of a club that I didn't make it into and that was the excuse I told myself for many years. The problem, aside from reinforcing the belief that I didn't have what it takes to be successful, was that nothing changed. I was totally on the effect side of life, blaming my genetics for where I'd ended up and I can promise you that digging the hole of reasons why it wouldn't work for me only made it a bigger hole to get out of. My RAS kept presenting me with all the evidence I needed to prove it was true and how to keep it in place.

The good news is that motivation isn't something you are either born with or without; it's something we all have. It's just not necessarily driven by the things we like or would like to achieve.

Let's start by looking at where our motivation actually comes from. This is based on the work of the late Dr Tad James, the creator of Time Line Therapy® and Dr Adriana James, both Master Trainers and experts in the field of NLP hypnotherapy and coaching. Now, believe it or not, the things that motivate us as adults are mostly in place before we reach the tender age of around 10 years old, if not sooner. Back when you were young, you were a little unconscious mind absorbing the world around you, with no conscious mind critically looking at the information you were taking in. The rational, logical filter we have as adults hadn't developed up to that period and so we just accept what we were told to be true and important.

Our well-intended parents, teachers, friends, grandparents, siblings, culture, even fictional TV or book characters, all influence our views of the world, even without words.

Behaviour speaks volumes!

The way a person behaves is a direct reflection of what is important to them. The things that are important to us are our values – the true motivators for everything we do as people.

The thing with values is that they aren't simply those things we aspire to have. If only it were that straightforward...

"I want to be successful and make money, therefore I am naturally driven to do the things that will help me achieve that."

If values worked in that way, then we would all achieve every-thing we ever wanted. Wanting something to be important, to be motivated by that very thing, doesn't make it so. Our values are not something we consciously decide.

Our values reside in our unconscious mind, the submarine!

The way to spot someone's true unconscious values is by how they spend their time. Our values are quite literally the things we value and so we put them first.

If someone says exercise is important, yet they never make the time to do any, you can assume it's probably not a value of theirs, even if they want it to be. If it were truly something they value highly, they would prioritise exercise over other things. The people who always make time to exercise, no matter what else is going on in life, have exercise high up there in their hierarchy of values; they highly value it.

Before I knew about values, I used to say that money was important to me and I wanted to make lots of it... How very aspirational of me! Don't get me wrong, I did want to make money. Who doesn't? But the behaviour I carried out did not reflect the words I said and behaviour is the most important thing. I was very good at talking about things like I meant them, but actions speak louder than words. The minute something more appealing, more important than making money, came up, I was off. Talking the talk is not the same as walking the walk!

Whether it's money, exercise, study, relationships, travel or anything else for that matter, being high up on the list of values is neither good nor bad; it's only an issue when you want something, but that very thing is not important to you at the unconscious level. When the thought of actually taking action to do the thing you want to do doesn't make you want to get out of bed in the morning and you're not motivated to find time for it, regardless of whatever else is going on in life – and there will always be other things going on in life – then it can be a problem. There's a conflict between a conscious desire and an unconscious drive to achieve it, which creates friction.

Values also form our moral compass and what we use to judge the difference between right and wrong. If someone acts in a way that violates our values, then we will feel negative emotions. They are there as a guide for us to know and enforce our own personal boundaries and without them, we wouldn't know what is deemed acceptable or not. For example, if someone highly values thoughtfulness in a relationship and their partner behaves in a way that they see as being unthoughtful towards them, they will feel negative emotions. If this happens, it's important to let the other person know that it's not okay and enforce your boundaries, or let it go. When people neither address it nor forget about it, the emotion remains and often grows stronger, bubbling away in the background like a saucepan about to boil over!

Whilst I've given a couple of examples, it's important to note that values aren't limited to exercise and making money; they span across all areas of life and everything we do. I'm talking relationships, health, fitness, career, personal development, marriage, sex, travel, life... The list goes on!

Values are high-level, ambiguous words, such as security,

freedom, flexibility, fun, variety, respect, happiness, excitement, love, achievement and recognition, that encompass a whole lot of meaning within them. The reason a particular value is important and the meaning of the word itself, will be different for each person. Honesty in relationships to one person may mean knowing about their partner's past, their plans for the future and where the relationship fits in with those plans. Someone else's representation of honesty may be that they express their feelings to each other openly and often. Every person is an individual and no two minds work in the same way.

Back to motivation and where it comes from. When growing up, you absorb the unconscious messages you were receiving, so even if the values of those surrounding you weren't verbalised as being important, the seeds will have been planted in your young brains as you observed behaviours and imprinted those values in your own mind.

Here's the thing: times change and we also change as people, so the values that were instilled back then are more than likely out of date, or they just simply don't work for us and our goals now, but the brain is still programmed to be motivated to fulfil those same things. It would be like using a Sat Nav from when you were five years old and expecting it to get you to your destination today. You just wouldn't do it, because you'd accept there to be a high probability that the Sat Nav would no longer be effective at getting you there. Many of the roads will have changed; new roads will have been added and the chances you'll arrive in the time predicted are highly reduced, if you manage to get there at all.

The mind is just the same. The programming that was installed back when you first came into this world is not the latest version available to you and because we are all different, with different goals and dreams, with different experiences along the way, that initial programming isn't necessarily the best for you.

Whilst I am all for encouraging everyone to take full responsibility for their life and everything in it, we can't actually take full credit for our values, because they aren't really our own – we inherited them. What we can do is take full responsibility for what we do next. Moaning that something isn't working and doing nothing to change it is a good way to feel stuck, whilst irritating yourself and others. This isn't me lecturing in any way. I was that person for a long time. It was when I got bored with the sound of my own voice and listening to all the reasons why life wasn't working as I would like that I knew something had to give.

Our values are not set in stone... hooray! If you don't like them or they are not going to get you where you want to go in life, then you can change them. Without taking action towards this, the values we develop during those early years can often stay in place for life. That is, unless we experience an emotional event along the way, which all of us will do at some point.

When these events occur, the emotions associated with them can be either what you could call good or bad and the significance of those emotions will be different for each person. This could include anything from failing an exam, losing a job, having a baby, getting married, or even breaking a leg. It can even include events that don't affect you personally, but that have emotion connected to them, such as 9/11, Covid-19 and the lockdowns, recessions and other local, national or even global events.

There aren't any rules about what these events must be and how much emotion must be felt for them to change your values. When they do change, the things that used to be important to you no longer are; your perception is altered and new things make their way up your values hierarchy. You only have to look at people who have recently had a baby as an example of how values in every area of life can change in an instant. The minute that little bundle of joy comes into the world, everything changes. All the things that used to be the most important in the world become irrelevant; priorities change and the motivation to fulfil those old things just isn't there anymore. But without those emotional events or doing intervention work with a professional coach to purposefully make changes, many of our values have the potential to stay in place throughout our lives.

Your values reside in your unconscious mind, the submarine. So, if the submarine is programmed and motivated to go north and the things you want are facing south, then it will feel like you're rowing against the tide because, metaphorically, you are. The first step is to know which direction the submarine is pointing in.

I will say this again, as it's why many people give up and revert to their old, ingrained behaviours and the reason why their life isn't what they want it to be. Whilst you may not be responsible for the values that were passed down to you, you are responsible for what you choose to do next!

Just knowing that your values are the drive behind your motivation, or lack thereof, is empowering. You need to understand what isn't working in order to change it.

Time to get to know yourself a little better!

Activation Tool – Core Driver Discovery

Choose which area is of most importance to you right now, the one that impacts your life the most. The one that, if changed, would also have the biggest impact on all the other areas of life, too. Some examples are career, relationship, business, spirituality, health and fitness, family and friends.

Before you begin this exercise, remember that values are ambiguous words and phrases that have very little detail, such as freedom, happiness, security, protection and love. Each person's values will mean something different to them.

The key to carrying out this exercise effectively and really tapping into your unconscious mind is to do it quickly, writing whatever comes to mind and to keep writing until you have nothing left to write.

Get yourself a notepad and make a list of your answers to the following questions:

- **What is important to you about [insert the area of impor-tance, e.g. career]?**

Keep writing your list of the words that come to mind until you can't think of anything else.

Remember that these are not the things that you want; they are the things that are important to you right now, even if you don't like them or wish they weren't important.

Once you have finished, ask yourself the following question:

- **What else is important to you about [insert the same area]?**

Go! Write whatever comes to mind. Once you have finished, ask yourself one more time.

- **What else is important to you about [insert the same area]?**

Write anything that is left until you have listed everything important to you in that area.

You should have at least eight values on the list by now. If not, ask yourself again until you do. Some of the values may be different words but mean the same thing, e.g. 'stability' and 'being grounded'. In this case, you can group these words together.

· **Rewrite the list in order of importance, starting from the most important value down to the least important.**

Again, do this quickly. Your values live in your unconscious mind, so any analysis is your conscious mind kicking in.

What do you do if you're unsure which is the most important (because they are all important, right!)?

Ask yourself, out of the ones where you can't decide which to put first, if you could only have one of them in your life, which would it be? Once you've chosen, move to the next value on the list and do the same thing. There will probably be some values that initially feel equally important, but there will always be one that has the edge. Trust your unconscious mind and whatever you think the answer is, go with that.

By this point, you will have a list of your values, your motivators in the area you chose to focus on first. This list should give you a good indication as to why you are where you are and the results you have created.

I did this process when I left a very unhealthy, almost 10-year relationship and it explained a lot! I had overcome so many obstacles to leave the relationship and in doing so, I thought that all my issues had disappeared and I was ready for the world of dating!

What I quickly realised was that whilst I may have broken through the barriers of leaving the relationship, the things I held of value were still very much driven by the experiences I had been through. I was attracting different faces in different places, but the same patterns were presenting themselves to me. I had spent years not valuing myself and seeing myself as being less than other people, undeserving of having a loving relationship and the men I started dating reflected that back to me. They appeared to feel the same way about me as I did about myself.

The world is a mirror reflecting back at you.
You'll only find love to the extent you are willing to love yourself.

The things that were important to me were all based on what I didn't want. Let me explain what I mean by that.

Our values motivate us, but the energy behind each of our values and the reasons they are important to us is one of the biggest causes of why the motivation does or doesn't last.

The energy and motivation behind each of our values is either driven towards what is wanted, which is all about the good stuff we'll get from them, or away from what is not wanted – the things we want to avoid in life.

I remember when I first heard this, I thought that it was obvious that my motivation was towards all the good stuff. I didn't want any of those unwanted things in life, so surely they wouldn't motivate me.

Well, it turns out it's not quite that simple.

The very fact that I knew that I *didn't* want them was a good indication that I was pushing against something.

Motivation to Avoid Pain

The motivation to not have pain is driven by the avoidance of the very thing you don't want and it's not always obvious that it's happening. It's not about excitedly feeling inspired to run in the direction of your goals; it's about not feeling the pain of its opposite.

We have experiences that cause us to feel negative emotions, anything from a health scare, not having enough money, being hurt by someone, or being made redundant. An event happens that causes us to feel a negative emotion in the moment that we don't want to experience again. The reason we feel a negative emotion in those instances is that the event or experience is something that goes against our values. If someone values security in their career and they are threatened with redundancy, this will more than likely bring negative feelings to the surface, because their values are no longer being met; they are under threat. That can be the motivation for that person to take action to avoid what they don't want to happen.

Not only that, but those events also have the potential to change our values. In a previous relationship, my then-partner cheated on me and the things I valued and felt driven to look for changed. Overnight, things such as honesty, trust and monogamy became very important to me – things that, previously, I hadn't given any thought to.

Here's the critical part: the reason they became important to me was because I didn't want to experience the same emotions that made them a priority in the first place. The motivation behind my seeking honesty, trust and monogamy was driven by the anger, the sadness, the hurt I felt and the fear that I would be cheated on again in the future.

This was also true of my health on a smaller scale. I didn't like the way I looked and so I was motivated to exercise and eat healthily. Yes, of course, I wanted to look and feel a certain way, but the reason and drive behind it was because I didn't want to stay as I was; I wanted to get away from the body I didn't like.

Imagine you're walking through a tunnel.

At one end, there's a bright light – everything you want lives there: success, fulfilment, achievement and the kind of performance you know you're capable of.

At the other end, it's dark – filled with everything you're desperate to avoid: failure, pressure, self-doubt, missed chances.

When you commit to elevating your performance - whether in sport, business, or life - you have to start somewhere. For most high achievers, that place isn't the highlight reel; it's the low point. The pressure, frustration, feeling fed up with knowing you're underperforming, stuck, or capable of more.

Knowing what you don't want brings the opposite into focus: what you do want. That tension, the gap between current reality and your potential, often fuels the desire for change and kicks things into gear. It creates contrast and contrast creates hunger.

So, you start at the dark end of the tunnel, where things feel heavy or off-track. You're not where you want to be and because it doesn't feel good, you have a strong motivation to move - to take steps backwards, away from it. You're motivated to avoid the things that live in the darkness. You begin creating distance.

As you do, the light behind you begins to brighten the tunnel. With each step, the tunnel gets lighter and lighter. You gain some breathing room. There's relief - the pain starts to fade.

The motivation to avoid pain does have its benefits. There is a lot of energy behind it. It's something you really don't want in your life, so it's a powerful way to kick-start momentum to take action, but there are two main reasons why it doesn't last.

Reason #1: The pain wears off!

You've survived! The very thing that motivated you in the first place is now a distant memory and so it doesn't feel so bad. The pain has worn off.

A little bit of discomfort is tolerable and so few people take action when things are okay. It's only when something is painful enough that there is a reason to change it. Think of it like wearing shoes that are a little too tight. A couple of hours wearing them whilst sitting down is not ideal, but it is doable and so many people would be willing to put up with that level of pain. If those same shoes had to be worn on a 10-mile hike, then the motivation to change them would be totally different.

After two days of eating takeaways and drinking more wine than I care to share with you, it was painful. I was tired, bloated, sluggish; my head was foggy, I felt depressed, my trousers felt tight, I ached all over and everything generally felt like hard work. I felt like I had metaphorically, or even physically, taken myself for a 10-mile hike in a pair of shoes that were two sizes too small. Roll forward five days, after eating well and exercising. The bloating had deflated, my trousers didn't feel so tight and I'd caught up on my sleep, so I was far enough away from the problem, the very thing that kick-started the motivation to be healthy in the first place. The drive to continue exercising and eating well became less and less, until it would eventually wear off completely. It would start with *"just the one"* and *"I deserve a treat,"* which eventually spiralled into a weekend of taking it to the extreme. It was only then, after yet another Saturday and Sunday of eating junk food like it was going out of fashion, with the promise that *"I'll start again on Monday"*, that it would begin to feel painful enough again and the motivation would kick back in!

Like everything in life, it's not limited to one area, because we tend to take ourselves with us. This is something that can often be witnessed in business when someone is driven to set up their own company to get away from a job, a salary or a boss they don't want. When starting in a new company, money may be in short supply and so the new business owner buckles up and does what they need to do to bring sales in. When things are tight and not going well, or how they want them to, there's a lot of motivation to knuckle down and get stuff done. They are avoiding the pain of not feeling secure, of not having enough money to pay the bills, to keep a roof over their head and eat. They may want to avoid being in a position where they are not respected or they don't feel free, all the things that created the drive to start the business. They work hard to make sure all those things don't come to fruition. The frustration, the fear and the hurt that led to their decision to set up on their own in the first place keep them going. They take action consistently; they work hard and eventually they get results and there is money in the bank; the sales targets have been met; they can pay the bills and maybe even splash out a little.

Phew, relief!

They are out of the danger zone; they have successfully avoided the things they didn't want and so they take a breath, ease their foot off the gas and relax for a while. They can afford to – there's enough money to keep them going and they have worked hard, so they deserve a rest. They have the day off, treat themselves to something new and shiny and enjoy the rewards of their labour. After some time has passed, the positive results they had been getting start to dwindle again. They stopped doing the very thing that caused them to achieve the sales, the activities that brought the money into the business in the first place and so they dried up and so did the money. For every effect, there is something that caused it. In this case, the work they were doing caused the sales and when the work slowed down or stopped, so did the sales that followed. Eventually, it becomes painful enough again. The money is running out and so the motivation kicks in and they get that booty into action. It's the boom-and-bust cycle and unless something changes, it can repeat itself time and time again, over a whole lifetime. This is a common underlying cause of inconsistent performance.

Now picture yourself again, standing in that tunnel with the dark end in front of you and the light shining from behind. You're walking backwards, further and further away from the darkness, the unwanted. With each step, it becomes a little brighter and feels less painful.

But walking backwards is exhausting – it's simply not how we're built to move, so you take a break and allow yourself to take just a few steps forward... what harm could it do? You're still far from the dark.

Step by step, little by little, you slowly drift back into the dark, back to where you started. Until it becomes painful enough, you want to get away and so the cycle repeats.

It's a never-ending cycle of going backwards and forwards like a yo-yo, without reaching peak performance before the momentum runs out. This inconsistency takes a lot of mental, physical and emotional energy and usually doesn't take you to where you really want to go.

Reason #2: It has no direction!

When something is painful or unwanted in life, the focus is on being anywhere but there. In that moment, it doesn't matter where you are going as long as it gets you away from the place you don't want to be.

When I first started dating after 10 years of being off the market, it was important to me that I found someone with whom I felt secure, because I didn't want to get hurt again. I looked for people whom I believed would be honest because I was scared I was going to be lied to. I was motivated to find someone who wouldn't treat me poorly, like I didn't matter or I wasn't worthy of being with them and I was happy to consider anyone who didn't display those traits or behaviours. The problem with that is I wasn't taking steps to look for what I actually wanted in a relationship, because the truth was, I had no idea. My time was spent making sure that men didn't meet the criteria of unwanted things, without giving much time and thought, if any, to deciding where I was headed next.

Think of it a bit like being close to a fire that is too hot. Who cares where you end up, as long as you don't get burnt! This can be a good thing at first because it stops you from feeling the heat, so it feels less painful. Here's the issue: the desire to avoid something is directionless. You're not heading towards anywhere; you're just moving away from where you don't want to be without a place to go in mind. It becomes about surviving the heat, so anywhere is good as long as it's not hot anymore. When you begin to cool off, you may find that you don't like where you've ended up.

When you jump in your car and pull out your Sat Nav, you have to input the destination you want to go to. Asking your Sat Nav to take you away from where you currently are doesn't work. It doesn't know where to direct you. Your mind works in just the same way.

Although you will begin to move away from the thing you don't want, your focus is still on it. Remember that you get what you focus on, whether you want it or not. Without choosing where you want to end up, the Sat Nav is programmed to point in the direction of where you currently are and so you keep ending up back there.

You're back in the tunnel, standing at the dark end with the light behind you. You start stepping away, but without a clear destination, you drift into one of the side tunnels. You didn't choose it because you wanted to be there, only because you didn't want the darkness.

You're still walking backwards, spending all your energy avoiding what you don't want, without ever turning to face where you do want to go. Eventually, it gets exhausting. How can you stay motivated when you have no clear target? Your focus stays on the dark end, because that's all you can see.

After a while, you stop to rest. A few steps forward feel harmless, even comfortable. But step by step, almost without noticing, you find yourself right back where you started.

When you unconsciously make the decision to avoid something, your energy is used to do just that. But even when you're far enough away from it that it's no longer painful, your attention is still on it.

"What you resist, persists!"
  Carl Jung

When you're still pointing your attention and focus in the direction of the unwanted without realising it, as the motivation gradually fades, you begin to make your way back towards it until it becomes painful again and the motivation kicks in... again. A life of what you are NOT going to do leads to self-sabotage because you get what you focus on.

Motivation to Thrive

Turning your attention towards having the motivation to thrive is where it's at. This type of motivation has direction. It's focused on and driven towards the things that you want.

When I decided to deal with the past baggage I had been carrying around from my previous relationship and even before that, I was surprised and delighted by the things that then became important to me and how my focus changed.

When the hurt, fear, anger, sadness, guilt and the beliefs I held about myself and my worth were resolved, the values I had once had around honesty, respect, monogamy and so on all changed. My values became such wonderful things that had previously been out of my awareness. I valued love, happiness, fun, laughter and connection and these values were all driven towards the pure desire to enjoy them. I was no longer running from the things I felt were lacking in my life or things I was worried would happen if I didn't have certain things present.

To give you just one example, trust in relationships was always high up in the things I valued in the past and it was because I didn't want someone I couldn't trust - negative emotions were driving it. I had experienced mistrust and was still wearing the scars. In fact, the wounds hadn't healed; the emotional cuts were still raw and this was obvious in the choices I made and the way I approached potential relationships. I had my guard up because I was afraid I would be hurt again. It caused such inner turmoil for me because I wanted to find love and be happy, but at the same time, I didn't want to let my guard down. I had a deep internal conflict and it showed up in my behaviour - like two parts of me were pulling in opposite directions. Part of me wanted to find someone, but the other part of me didn't. I was unconsciously protecting myself on some level. I'd go all in at the start, then as soon as that was reciprocated and getting close was on the cards, I'd back off and push them away. Talk about mixed messages!

When I finally released the conflict and the emotion behind the values, trust was no longer important. I no longer had any reason not to trust; it became irrelevant. I felt like I was able to breathe again!

I fully appreciate that not everyone is in the position right now to work with a professional coach and deal with the past and the emotions that go with it. If you are, I would be more than happy to recommend some amazing coaches who have the tools to release inner conflicts, past negative emotions and beliefs quickly, some of whom I have trained personally. If you're not able to right now, or if it's not for you, that's okay too. You can certainly begin to make changes by completing the exercises in this book. Just adjusting the direction of your focus alone will have a big impact on where that takes you and the consistency needed to get there.

You're in the tunnel, darkness ahead, light behind. You realise that walking backwards isn't taking you far and worse than that, all you see is darkness; so you stop, decide what you truly want and turn to face towards it – towards the light.

The tunnel brightens and a winding path appears, leading towards everything you desire. The dark end is still there, but it's behind you now. It no longer drives you – instead, the pull of your vision does.

You're grateful for the experiences you've had in the darkness because without them, you wouldn't know there is light; it gave you clarity. The difference now is that your focus is ahead of you, in the light and you feel pulled towards it. It's no longer about looking at the dark in an effort to leave it behind; it's about the shiny future in front of you, the things that are to come that you know are yours and you deserve!

Time to turn that focus around!

Activation Tool – Value Realignment Reset

You have your list of values from the previous activation point. If you haven't completed this yet, do that first before you continue with this exercise.

Go through your list of values one at a time and ask yourself the following questions, writing down your answers as you do:

· **What positive things can I learn from the experiences I**

have had that made this value important to me? What can I learn that will help me in the future?

Do this for each value before carrying on. *For example,*

Value: *Honesty*

Learning: *It's okay to go with the flow; I can trust in myself.*

Value: *Security*

Learning: *I can choose what actions I take; I'm in control of how I show up for myself.*

· **Going through each value again, with the new positive learning you now have, ask yourself:**

If I knew this value was a given, that I just knew it was taken care of, what would I really want? What does that mean – how will I know I have it?

Write down everything that you want, even if you have no idea how you will get it.

For example,

Honesty – if I knew this was a given, then I would want

Fun

Fun = having hobbies we enjoy doing together

*Security – if I knew this was a given, then I would want **Freedom***
   Freedom = supporting each other's dreams and goals

Pretending that you don't want something when you do doesn't make the desire go away. Be honest with yourself and enjoy it!

This is about deciding how you want your life to be, so it should light you up when you think about it.

Once you've done this, it's time to check your focus.

· **Re-read the things you have just written down, the things you want. Check if there is anything in there that is focused on not having something you don't want.**

The giveaways and words to look out for are... "I won't..."

"I no longer..."
   "I don't..."
   "I haven't..."
   "I'm not..."
   "I have less..."
   "I have enough..." - This is a sneaky one. Having enough of something is based on lack and scarcity; it essentially covers the basics. Rather than 'enough', what do you actually want?

· **Notice where your focus and attention go when you read it. What picture comes to mind?**

Any values that are driven by avoidance will face the dead end of the tunnel; these are the things you want to get away from. Even if the image of what you don't want only flickers into your mind for a moment, it's still there.

Flip it by asking, What is the opposite of it?

The drive to thrive feels good! It feels expansive and energising. The feeling of avoiding pain is not energising; it feels draining and restrictive. Become familiar with the difference you feel internally between the two. This is feedback for what is going on unconsciously in the submarine of your mind, even when your conscious mind in the rowing boat isn't sure if it's heading in the right direction or not.

There are many ways to take a deeper dive into what is going on in the depths of your mind and I encourage you to do that whenever possible.

Your external world is filtered through your unconscious mind, which is the home of your beliefs, emotions, memories, view of energy, time, values, personality type and several other factors. When you make changes at the unconscious level, when you release the negative emotions and limiting beliefs that drive your motivation, you are essentially changing the lens that you see the world through and so the world you see changes. Your internal filters change, which automatically adjusts the information you delete, distort and generalise from your experience. The outside world is a mirror of your internal world and when one changes, the other is altered too. For physical creation to take place outside of you, the change to get there must happen inside first.

Tuning into and listening to yourself, getting to know what those unconscious filters are, is a great starting point and something you can do straight away today.

8

Fail to Accelerate Growth

Failure is a greater teacher than success."
  Clarissa Pinkola Estés

Getting things "wrong" is often the quickest way to success!

I remember listening to an interview with the founder of Spanx, Sara Blakely, who said that every evening after school, her dad would ask her what she had failed at that day. When I first heard this, I thought it was a very bizarre concept, but when I began to really understand failure, it made total sense.

The easiest way to not fail is to not do anything, to not push yourself, to not do the things you don't already know, to not go outside of what's comfortable, to not do anything you feel uncertain about.

It's also the quickest way to prevent yourself from achieving what you want

Think back to the first time you tried tying your shoelaces. I imagine you probably weren't successful and if you did manage to get the laces to stay together, you probably didn't achieve the perfect bow. At that age, you also likely didn't apply any meaning to the experience, whether you managed to tie your shoelaces or not. We know that not being able to tie shoelaces doesn't mean that a person is a complete failure. Just like not coming first in the egg-and-spoon race on sports day doesn't mean that the child will never achieve anything when they grow up and failing a maths exam doesn't mean that the person will never make any money. Of course it doesn't! Failing at one thing does not mean anything. Whilst this is understood logically, when it comes to taking action towards our goals as adults, that logic seems to get lost.

Not getting things right the first time can be frustrating; even at a young age, we want to get that shoelace tied on the very first attempt. But as children, we expect to mess up and we don't attach identity or meaning to the failure. As adults, that's where things change. We begin attaching meaning to mistakes and that's where the problem begins. We start making the failure mean something about us, rather than seeing it as part of the process.

Setting up a new business and not getting sales in the first month of trading does not mean the business won't work and that the business owner will never be successful. Missing the podium in the first competition of the season doesn't mean you've lost your edge. Going on dates with six potential partners and not meeting someone suitable for a second date does not mean that the individual is unlovable and destined to be alone forever. Eating too much chocolate on a Saturday night does not mean a person's diet is totally ruined and they will always be overweight. High-level performance isn't linear and one off-day is not a prediction of long-term failure - it's feedback, not a forecast.

The same principle applies in reverse, too. Setting up a business and only working on it for a month does not make a successful business. Going on a date once does not make a loving relationship. Eating healthily one night a week is not how you lose weight. If you followed these guidelines, you would probably expect to fail.

Remember the Law of Cause and Effect and the idea that nothing happens without a cause. This is especially useful to keep in mind when things don't go as planned. Missing a goal, underperforming in a competition, or hitting a setback doesn't mean you're doomed to fail - it simply means there's a cause behind the result. It's feedback, not finality. Instead of assigning heavy meaning to the outcome ("I'm not good enough," "It's over"), this law invites you to zoom out and ask: *What cause created this effect? And what could I shift next time?*

Another law that plays a big role here is the Law of Rhythm, which reminds us that everything moves in cycles - highs and lows, expansions and contractions. Even the most elite athletes, entrepreneurs and creators experience fluctuations in energy, motivation, performance and results. When you're in a dip, it doesn't mean you've lost your edge; it means you're in a natural rhythm. The key is to trust that the upward swing will come and to stay grounded during the downward curve, staying focused on your outcome. This is an opportunity to recommit to yourself and your goals, which is when inner strength is built.

Also worth remembering is the Law of Polarity, which tells us that everything has an opposite. Every perceived "failure" contains the seed of growth, insight and redirection. Without contrast, success wouldn't even be recognisable. What feels like a breakdown now might later reveal itself as the turning point you needed.

Even though the concept of failure is understood, so many people will actively avoid it to the point that they don't pursue the things they want.

Why is failure something that is feared?

I remember being in my early thirties and applying to be the lead singer in a band. It wasn't something I'd ever wanted to do before, but I thought it would be good fun and a nice addition to the acting and modelling work I was doing at the time. The funny thing was that I had no real singing experience. I hadn't had any singing lessons and wasn't really sure if I sounded good. All I knew was that I loved karaoke and I had received many compliments over the years, although it was coming from people who had usually had a lot to drink, so their judgment probably wasn't a useful gauge of whether or not I had any real talent. When I applied for the audition, I didn't think I would actually get it, so I didn't give it much thought beyond the application...

... until the email landed in my inbox!

We would like to see you next Tuesday at 3pm for your audition. Please prepare x, y and z songs.

I was invited to sing three different songs that included a mixture of range and styles, so they would be able to hear my vocal ability and see how I performed. I remember that one of the songs was a big number by Mariah Carey, something that would stretch even those with the best voices. Whilst I was able to use the mindset tools I had learnt to clear up any limiting beliefs about myself and give me the confidence I needed, I also knew that believing I had a voice that matched some of the world's greatest didn't mean that I actually did. Just like believing I am an amazing driver doesn't make me Lewis Hamilton. There would need to be some practiced skill thrown into the mix, too. Working only on the mental plane of existence doesn't magic things into existence.

On the afternoon of the audition, I practiced the songs I was going to sing. I visualised myself having completed them and being really pleased with my performance, as the people auditioning me said how great I was. I was having such fun doing it, singing into my hairbrush like a diva, throwing around some dance moves and thinking I was the next Lady Gaga, when I suddenly found myself thinking about the fact that I may not get it. I could fail. Then what? What would that mean?

I started questioning myself. Who was I to audition? I had no experience. I was a fraud! If I went for it and didn't get it, that would just prove to me that I wasn't good enough and I didn't have what it takes. Any positive beliefs I had could be shattered if someone who knew more than I did told me I didn't have the talent, the look, the X factor. I suddenly felt scared!

The interesting thing is that in those few seconds, nothing had actually changed in the world, yet I went from having fun and feeling excited to not having fun and feeling fearful in an instant. The experience I was having in that moment and the experience I would continue to have if I carried on feeling that way were completely altered by the meaning I had applied to it – me not being accepted into the band would mean I have no talent and I'm not good enough.

I very quickly found myself coming up with all sorts of reasons and excuses as to why I probably shouldn't bother going for the audition, finding problems that didn't even exist to rationalise my thinking. I decided that I may not be able to work on all the dates they want, I'm not sure that I like all of the songs they play; I'd probably end up having to work most Saturday nights and I don't think I want to do that; I don't know the other people in the band and we may not get on; maybe I shouldn't bother after all. I worked my way through at least 15 excuses to not go for it in the space of 30 seconds.

Then I sat with it for a few minutes to think about what was really going on.

I very quickly realised that, up to that point, all I'd really done was think about being in a band as something that I might do one day, which was fun. There was no pressure involved because it wasn't really happening, so I couldn't fail. Whereas the thought of actually putting myself in the position where I would actually be doing it – I would be singing in front of people and they would be judging me on my performance and deciding if I was good enough to join them or not – well, that was something different entirely. Beyond that, I could be performing in front of crowds of people who may not like what I have to offer. It meant that failing was possible!

My logic was that if I didn't do it, then I wouldn't fail. I could create reasons and excuses as to why I didn't pursue it in the first place and tell myself that was the reason it didn't happen, not because I failed. I couldn't fail at something that I didn't even try, which certainly felt like the safer option, the way to protect myself. By not putting myself in a position where I could be rejected, I wouldn't be. If I didn't do it, I wouldn't fail. But it also meant that I wouldn't succeed. Not succeeding because I didn't go for it would actually be the biggest failure of all.

Embracing Failure

I personally choose the belief that failure doesn't exist. In my world, not achieving something I set out to do is feedback so I can adapt and do it differently in the future. For this section, I'm going to use the word 'failure' so you know what I'm referring to and how you can reframe and use it to benefit you.

Our unconscious mind is designed to protect us and so if it perceives something as a threat, it will look for ways to prevent it from happening. When we see not being successful at something as failure, our unconscious mind kicks in to keep us safe; it's doing its job. The problem is that whilst the intention is good, the result isn't always desirable.

To stop this from happening, you need to get your unconscious mind on board so that it knows you are safe and no longer feels the need to step in when you think things may not work out. To do that, it's about reframing what failure means to you. It's time to break down the reality of failing!

Failure is quite simply a **F**uture **A**ttempt **I**n **L**earning **U**ntil **R**eality **E**xists.

You are attempting to do something that will be a reality in the future, right now, which will cause you to learn in the process. Once you have done it, that very thing becomes your reality.

You can spend all day, every day learning the theory of something; you can become the world's most versed in your knowledge about the subject, but no amount of knowledge will outweigh what you will gain through the experience of it. You can read about swimming and how to do it; you can watch videos on it, learn about all the different strokes, how to have the best form and make yourself go faster, yet the only way to really know it is to do it. Even with all of the knowledge about it, you'll probably never feel ready to actually go and do it in practice. Knowing and doing are very different things. Jumping in the pool is the only real way you will learn to swim and of course, no matter how much theory you know about swimming, you wouldn't expect to get it right on your first attempt, which is why armbands and floats were invented.

Better to make mistakes, say and do things that don't work, instead of waiting until you have it all figured out. Even if it doesn't work, you'll learn along the way until eventually something does. You may even find that in doing it, it isn't what you thought it would be and so it gives you clarity.

I should mention that even when you know this stuff, you're still human and there will always be those unconscious pat- terns that need breaking to propel you forward, so it's better to get used to it and see the opportunity to grow than to wish away what could make for an interesting ride.

It's easy to put something off until you believe it's perfect or you are ready, but the reality is that you will never feel ready to do something for the first time. How can you be ready to do something you don't know? The quickest and the only way to become ready is to do it, just get started from wherever you are and work it out as you go. Fear of getting it wrong is usually what stops people from even beginning and it's almost always about other people. Fear of what they will think, what they will say, how they will judge you if it doesn't work out as planned. If someone wants to criticise you for doing the things they are not doing, that is about them, not you. The world is a mirror reflecting back to you who you are and if others take

187

it upon themselves to notice the action you are taking with negativity, it's really a reflection of what they don't believe is possible or what they are not doing for themselves. When this happens, send them love and then choose who you spend your time with. Having a supportive environment is fundamental to your growth as it's the foundation of everything you do.

Going back to the example of tying your shoelaces... You know that a child has to get it wrong so that they understand how to do it right and the same goes for everything else, even as an adult. When you begin to see taking action as an attempt to learn something that will be your reality in the future, the pressure is off, as there is no expectation that you will know how to do it straightaway. Every time you take action, see it as practice, an opportunity to learn and improve, because the reality is that it is just that and it always will be. No matter how great you become at the things you desire, there is always more – it's a never-ending journey of growth and improvement.

Imagine if the Beatles sat back after creating their first album and never did anything different. They could've quite easily thought the music they knew and had already created worked and so there was nothing to change. Think of all the amazing songs we would've missed out on if they hadn't risked doing something unknown to them, unknown to the world. It goes without saying that some of the songs they wrote worked better than others in terms of their success. This didn't mean they failed; they just found ways that didn't work so wel,l and they used that information to write their next songs differently. You can't account for everyone's taste, so forget about other people.

Along with the Beatles, Sara Blakley's dad appeared to be a wise man. By encouraging Sara to fail at something every day, she had to go out and make mistakes. The quickest way to do that is by going into the unknown and doing the very things you don't know how to do, the ones you are usually avoiding, which you are more likely to fail at. By pushing yourself to fail, you let your unconscious mind know that it's okay to fail. It's safe. In fact, you are looking for ways to do it because it's positive. If you do the very thing that you failed at again and again, taking on the feedback about what to do differently next time or what to work on, then each time you do it in the future, the chances of failing become less until success becomes the reality.

The more you fail, the less impact each failure has. It's then no longer the big thing that we so often turn it into, because if it doesn't work, it can be done again. Hardly anyone is successful on their first go and if everyone were successful at everything the first time, then the world would be a pretty boring place, as there would be nothing to strive for. The real joy of achievement is in the pursuit of it. When you arrive, you are there and so it's the new normal and there becomes a new aim, something else that you want and will probably not achieve when you first start. Accept that no matter how far you go, there will always be failure because there is always something more to achieve.

Letting Go of Success

To let go of failure, you must also let go of success. When you hold on so tightly to success and you think it must look like, you push it away and close off your mind to all the possible ways to achieve it.

A problem that often presents itself in the pursuit of a particular outcome is when you need it as opposed to wanting it. When you *need* something, you push it away without realising - the emotional pressure narrows your perception and closes off possibilities. You only have to think of the person who is desperate for a partner and ends up putting off any suiters that come their way. The saying 'you can smell the desperation' is really about the energy that person is radiating. Just like when you are in the presence of someone who has a high, driven and focused energy vs a defeated, victim energy, you feel it. Desperation has its own energetic blueprint.

To create something you want, you also have to be okay with not having it.

This may sound contradictory, but the energy behind it makes all the difference. When you cling too tightly to a specific outcome, trying to force it, you unintentionally block everything else that could lead you there. If you really want something to the point that you want it too much, your mindset may well be driven by the lack of it. Your focus becomes rigid, to the exclusion of anything else, you miss the alternative pathways your RAS would normally reveal.

It repels rather than attracts.

This is important: when your attention is fixed on the outcome being one way, you unconsciously reject everything outside of what you desire, anything that is not that thing you want. The problem is that anything you reject or don't want must be in your awareness. By having the frame of mind that something *must* happen, you notice everything that is not that, in other words, what you don't want. Your unconscious mind is focused on and draws your attention to the many ways to create those very things. My audition for the band was one way of achieving my goal to sing for fun outside of just doing karaoke and I could quite easily fail. Failure in this instance was that I may not be accepted into that particular band and there was a reasonable chance of that happening. If I'd needed that audition to be successful and decided this was my only shot, it would've shifted my internal reality – the feelings I had about it, the images it created in my mind and how I turned up and performed. It makes the thing you want the answer and the truth is that the answer is already inside you and there are many ways to create the physical representation in your external world.

Keeping focused whilst having flexibility is one way to stay open. Your focus activates your RAS and flexibility shows you all the other routes to the destination you desire. I have witnessed many people in my life who have applied for the job they say they would love and who, when not invited for an interview following their first application, gave up and resigned themselves to the fact that they will never have the job they want, so there is no point even trying. They have gone on to spend their whole lives doing jobs they hate and moaning about the fact that they weren't even given the chance to interview for that one particular company. More often than not, they didn't even attempt a second go at an interview. They had all their eggs in one basket with a single route of getting there, which, when not successful on the first attempt, they saw as failure because it didn't work out as planned.

The things you want can come in many forms, many ways that we mere humans in our own world haven't even considered. When you realise and accept this as being true, you will also see there really is no such thing as failure. If one way doesn't work, there will always be another that does.

I love the story of the drowning man and it's a great metaphor to take on board. In case you haven't heard it, here is a short synopsis:

A man found himself trapped in his house after a flood made its way through the town where he lived. The man began praying to God to come and rescue him. As the water started to rise, his neighbour offered to help. He had a pick-up truck that was big enough to get them through the rising water and take them to safety. The man refused, telling his neighbour, *"I am waiting for God to save me."* And so his neighbour left him.

The floods were getting worse and the water started rising even higher. The man had to make his way up to the roof of his house. He was continuing to pray to God to save him when a boat passed by. The people on the boat shouted to the man to join them to head to safety, but again the man refused. He told them he was waiting for God to rescue him and so they carried on without him.

The man absolutely believed that God would come through and save him. He carried on praying as the water kept rising. A short while later, a helicopter flew by and the man heard a voice over a speaker, offering to throw him a ladder and take him to safety. Again, the man refused. He shouted to the voice from the helicopter that God was going to save him and so the helicopter flew away, leaving the man on the roof. Eventually, the water became too high; it swept the man away and he drowned.

As he arrived at the gates of heaven, he came face to face with God. He asked God why he had not saved him. He had believed with every fibre of his being that God would rescue him, but he had let him drown. God was confused by this question and told the man, *"I sent you a pick-up truck, a boat and a helicopter and you turned all of them away. What else could I have done?"*

Keep in mind, 'this or something better,' and always be open and flexible.

The trick is to make every failure count, turning it into a success!

Every time you experience a perceived failure, there is always something to learn, something you can improve upon next time. If you don't get the interview upon first application, how can you adapt your CV next time? Who else could you contact to connect with the company you love? What could you do that you haven't considered yet? What is it you love about that company that other companies may have? Which other companies offer the same things you love about that particular company? What is your purpose for wanting to achieve that outcome? The reason for doing it is so much bigger than the thing itself – that is just one way you can have it. Failure can be the most amazing gift to you if you choose to see it that way.

It was 2.45pm on Tuesday afternoon and I had arrived for my audition. I'd watched some YouTube videos about warming up my vocals beforehand, which I thought would be helpful, but I actually found my voice was starting to feel quite tired and I hadn't even started yet – oops! I saw the person who was auditioning before me finishing off her last song, the big one and oh my gosh, she was good.

At that moment, I could've quite easily decided there was no point even bothering because her voice was so much better than mine. She had clearly done this before, but during my reflection earlier that day, I had worked out that I had no idea what the band was actually looking for. I had been briefed about what they wanted me to do and what the band was about, but I didn't know what criteria they had in mind. That also meant that no matter what happened, I couldn't fail. I may be the best singer in the world, with amazing dance moves, but if they are looking for someone who looks a certain way, has a particular tone of voice, a vibe about them that I don't fit, then I probably won't be the one they choose. This doesn't mean I'm not good enough or not worthy or a failure; it just means this isn't the one for me right now and I can learn from the experience.

It came time for me to step up to the stage. There was a video camera pointing at me; the band was to the side, ready to play. I'd never played with a live band, by the way and two other band members were sitting in front of me, ready to judge. They told me which song to start with and the band counted me in.

From that point on, it was a bit of a blur. All I know is that I decided I would just completely enjoy myself and be totally me. Putting on a performance that was anything less than who I really was would be exhausting and very short-lived. I know there were times when my voice squeaked in places it shouldn't. I didn't hit the high notes in parts and I completely forgot the words during one song, but I made some up in their place. It was as if I'd had my very own karaoke night with a live band. I had the most fun ever and said my goodbyes, thanking them for giving me the opportunity to sing.

The following day, I received a call from the band members to let me know how I had done. The verdict: I had failed! I wasn't accepted into the band. Well, that's how I could've looked at it anyway. What they actually said was that my energy and enthusiasm were intoxicating and my performance was brilliant. They also said that they do have a few bigger songs they play regularly and my vocals just didn't seem up to it. They had concerns about how I would manage playing a 45-minute set. I really appreciated their feedback and agreed that I would struggle. I would've most likely lost my voice before the set had finished. I hadn't become the person I needed to be for that position and that was okay.

There really is no such thing as failure. There is always an opportunity to evaluate and learn from everything you do. It's easy to use experiences that didn't work out as planned as the reason to not keep going, maybe even blaming others for not having successfully achieved what you want, but that just guarantees staying stuck.

The other option is to take those experiences and decide what you will do differently next time, looking at how you can improve or adapt so that the same mistakes aren't made. I decided to book myself in for singing lessons because I knew my voice didn't have the power to continually sing for 45 minutes without becoming croaky. This helped me massively and I did go on to sing many times in front of an audience, with my very own slot and I enjoyed every second of it!

Success is how you choose to respond to and look at the inevitable failures. It is the very best way to grow because, without it, there is no feedback to improve upon. When you begin to see every failure as a way to propel yourself forward on your journey to success, failure truly becomes your best friend.

The biggest failures bring the biggest opportunities!

Activation Tool – Failure-to-Fuel Method

Time to go and fail (or should I say learn)!

Answer the following questions:

· **What have I been avoiding through the fear that I will fail?**

List all the things you want to do that you don't want to get wrong or mess up.

· **What would happen if I did fail?**

Get it out of your head! What is the worst-case scenario?

· **If that happened, then what?**

If the worst-case scenario were a reality, what would happen?

How would you handle it?

· **What are the positive things that could come from failing?**

How would doing it, regardless of whether it worked or not, improve your life?

Putting it into practice

If you knew you could never fail, what would you do differently?

· **Go and do it!**

Aim to fail at least once a day and learn from it. After every go, ask yourself the following questions:

· **What did I learn from it?**

Make sure the things you learn are positive. This isn't about criticising yourself; it's about looking at what worked, what didn't work and how knowing that information will benefit you to do better in the future.

· **What will I do differently next time?**

Take what you have learnt and decide how you will adapt and change what you do next time, knowing what you now know.

9

Momentum in Motion

"You don't have to be great to start, but you have to start to be great."
   Zig Ziglar

When we talk about the Law of Attraction, it's easy to forget that *attraction* isn't passive. Whether it's in sport, business, or any high-performance field, results don't just "show up" because you want them - they respond to your energy, your focus and most importantly, your *actions*. Think about the word itself: *attraction* contains the word action. You can visualise the win, hold the mindset and set powerful intentions – but unless that's paired with aligned action, you're just daydreaming. The law doesn't reward wishful thinking; it mirrors the signals you're putting out through your behaviour, habits and choices.

In the world of high performance, whether you're aiming for a personal best, landing a dream role, or elevating your business, you can't attract results from the sidelines. You have to be in motion – training, refining, showing up, adjusting. You have to put yourself in the spaces where opportunities can recognise you.

The same is true for every other area of life. In the world of relationships, you can't attract a partner if you're hiding away at home, never engaging with others, or emotionally unavailable. You have to show up, be seen, open and available for connection. Whether it's career opportunities, health, or anything else, attraction isn't just about visualising success; it's about embodying it, through how you think, feel and act.

Attraction is a two-way street!

Think of attraction like a magnet pulling itself towards all the things that are a match. Every result you desire has a certain frequency and when your energy is in sync with that frequency for a sustained period, you are no longer just working towards a goal – you're drawing it towards you. This is why the intensity of your feelings matters... the more intense the feeling, the more pull there is; the less intense the feeling, the less the pull. And the more pull, the faster the time to creation.

When you think about achieving a goal, maybe hitting a new performance level, landing a major opportunity, or stepping onto a bigger stage and you allow yourself to really feel what that would be like, you are drawing it to you, which means you have the possibility of bringing it into your physical reality. You're shifting your internal state to match the outcome you want. That emotional rehearsal sends a strong signal to your unconscious mind that this is your direction.

But if you stop there, if no action follows, it sends mixed messages to your unconscious mind.

It's like setting your Sat Nav and then refusing to drive the car. Your mind is ready to support the goal, but your behaviour is saying, "Actually, I'm not moving." That's confusing to your system, which slows the momentum.

To bring this to life: imagine an athlete who visualises winning, feels the pride of success, sees the podium in their mind... but then skips training, avoids feedback, or keeps playing small. That vision doesn't stand a chance. Without real-world movement, the opportunity can't meet you. You might as well be waiting for the result to knock on your door uninvited.

It's no different than declaring you want a relationship, picturing the connection, feeling the love and then never leaving the house. Unless your soulmate is the Amazon driver, you're not putting yourself in the path of what you're asking for.

The desire for what you want and the action you take towards it contradict each other. This can lead to internal conflicts and inconsistent signals in the energy you emit.

"I want it but..."

"... I'm not going out to meet someone."

"... it's not important enough for me to do anything about."

"... I'm not invested in achieving it."

"... I don't really believe it will happen, so there's no point trying."

Whilst you may not be consciously thinking these things, at an unconscious level, there will be something that is not in alignment with the things you say you want; therefore, the frequency you vibrate at is not a match. It may be that sometimes you believe it, but not other times and so it creates a pulling towards and then a pushing away from the things you want. This inconsistency may show up in your behaviour, because you are giving out different frequencies at different times, which slows down or even prevents physical manifestations from appearing in your life. As soon as your manifestations are nearby and ready to come into physical form, they get pushed back again and stay in the energy realm as a possibility.

Taking action shows your unconscious mind that you mean business. You're willing to play your part in the creation of the things you want, stepping into the possibilities that come your way to make them probabilities and then reality. Just think about how this takes place in day-to-day life as a metaphor: if you were to decide you wanted a certain body shape or size, or you wanted your garden to look a certain way, or you wanted to travel to a certain destination, you know that in all of these scenarios you would absolutely have to take action for it to be achieved. You would need to eat certain foods and exercise, do some digging, buy plants, mow the lawn, book a flight and find accommodation; they all require action. Not a single one of them will magically appear in your lap whilst you're sitting meditating. You have declared that you want those things and set the intention to achieve them. They are done in the quantum world of possibility. Your job is to focus on them and feel good about at least 51% of the time, even when the day-to-day of life throws itself at you, continually increasing that percentage of time and focus as you become more aligned every day. When you can focus on the reality you want more than you focus on your reality as it currently stands, the things you desire will come to meet you with ease. And to do that, you need to be there and ready to receive them. The life you are living right now is a manifestation of focus, the thoughts, beliefs, feelings and expectations you have had up to this point and that can be changed if it's not what you want!

Activation of Action

What action should I take and when?

Taking action isn't about having all the answers and the truth is, you won't have them all; it's about getting started. Imagine all the possibilities that could happen, all the ways you could receive the things you want. You couldn't possibly know what they are, so trying to plan the exact route to get where you want to go never works.

When you put your destination into your Sat Nav, you fully expect and trust that you will arrive at where you want to go. You may not know the entire route, just where you are starting and where you will end up. You also know there may be roadworks, diversions, traffic and any number of things that may take you off the intended track at times. This doesn't stop you from doing it anyway, knowing you'll eventually get there. Imagine how long it would take to get anywhere if you waited until you knew all the details of the journey you were taking before you left the house. If you had to look up every turn you were taking along the way, every pothole you may bump across and all the cars and people you could interact with. By the time you have the full plan ready to go, things will have changed and you'd have to go back to square one to plan the whole journey again.

It may sound ridiculous to even think that way about jumping in your vehicle and going from A to B, yet this is what many people do when it comes to taking action in other areas of their lives. Rather than just keying in the destination of where they want to go – in other words, setting the goal and intention and then getting started without knowing all the turns and potential obstacles that will inevitably come up along the way – they wait until they think they have all the answers, which of course they never do. It's only when you start moving that the answers present themselves.

When you do begin taking action, your frequency changes because you are taking those steps towards the outcome you desire. This directs your focus and sends signals to your unconscious mind of what is important... ACTIVATE THE RAS!

Your reticular activating system is alerted and its focus changes, bringing to your attention the next step to take, the next road to go down, routes you may not have otherwise noticed.

If you want to start a business and you begin taking action to attract new clients, your RAS filters out all of the irrelevant information and homes in on the answers that will lead you there. Whether that is the best marketing platform for you, the social media post you write that connects you with your potential clients, or the person who can help you with exactly what you need. All these things are able to enter through the gateway of your unconscious mind and be brought to the attention of your conscious mind. When they are brought into your awareness, they'll feel good because the frequency is a match with your outcomes and so you'll feel inspired.

When you feel inspired to take action, you are in alignment with the direction of your desires!

Inspired action isn't about getting busy doing things that feel hard. It's also not about everything being easy and not having to do the work. The universal Law of Cause and Effect states that for every effect, for everything that happens, there will have been a cause that preceded it. Applying this law to action means you can more accurately predict the chances of your success based on the input required to achieve the output desired and vice versa.

This consists of the mental and emotional factors – the thoughts you have, the internal conversations, the things that are important to you, the beliefs you hold to be true or not and the way you feel. Then there is your behaviour, the action that you take.

Taking action you feel rubbish about or believe won't work is like running in sand – it's hard work and you don't get anywhere quickly. It will feel like one step forward, two steps back and this will be evident in your energy, too. We've all known of someone, or even been that person ourselves, who makes you wonder why they are even bothering to do something, as all they do is moan about it, or their heart clearly isn't in it.

You know when someone says they are fine, but the feeling you get from them is the total opposite of fine? That is the energy and the message that is emitted when action is taken from that place and it makes it a slow and painful process. The message of 'this is hard work' creates and attracts more hard work!

When someone is coming at it from this place, it's easy to appreciate why many people avoid taking action. A life that isn't enjoyable without the belief that there will be any reward at the end of it doesn't feel very inspiring.

Inspired Action

Take action and do the things you feel inspired to do.

Inspired action is when you have that idea, you feel compelled to do something, you wonder whether you should pick up the phone to that person, the same thought keeps coming to mind, it feels aligned, even if it doesn't make sense right now.

As I sit here writing this chapter, it's 10.30pm on a Thursday. I've had a long week and I'm tired, but I feel inspired to sit down and just get the words out. I wasn't even sure what those words would be, but I knew that if I did what I felt inspired to do and write, they would come.

It would be so easy to think, *I'll wait until tomorrow after I've had a good night's sleep.* But I know, unless I wake up really early, my diary is full and once the day begins, I'll be fully focused on that. I also know the inspiration may not be there in the same way that it is right now. It would also be easy to think, *It's been a long and busy week and I deserve to sit on the couch and relax with a glass of wine* and most people would encourage me to do just that...

"Give yourself a break. You deserve it."

"You work hard. You need some time off."

"It's important that you get your rest."

"Do it at the weekend if you have an hour spare."

I'm sure many of these would be said with love and good intentions. The problem is that goals require action and that will probably feel uncomfortable at times. Whilst taking action may not be easy, it is often exactly what you need to do for the creation of what you desire to come to fruition.

There are varying scales of action. You may have heard this before and I've said it myself: you must take BIG ACTION! It usually is true that the bigger the action, the bigger the reaction or result you'll get. However, big action can sometimes lead to the creation of negative emotions. Someone quitting their job today to dive into a new business that they have barely even started could create big problems when it comes to the end of the month and they have no money to keep a roof over their head and food on the table. If they don't have the finances to support the essentials to live, then their belief system will be put to the test and more than likely fall short if it doesn't have the strength or evidence to support them in knowing they can do it.

I personally believe that action is about taking consistent steps every day, which lead to big results. I could sit here all night and write 30 pages of this book, but if that's all I do for six months, I won't get very far, whereas writing a page every day for six months will very quickly add up. It also creates the habit of doing it, so on those days where it would be easy not to bother, the mental muscle has been flexed enough times that it can do it more easily, plus there is momentum. My RAS notices the times and opportunities to fit in writing the book. It also makes me aware of the experiences that happen throughout my day, which I then feel inspired to write about. My RAS provides me with the content I am looking for.

With each step you take, you are tipping the scales in your favour, even if it doesn't feel like it at the time. Those incremental steps taken day by day, over time, add up to big dreams and the good part is that it is something we can all begin doing straightaway!

The more momentum you build internally, the more equipped you are to navigate the inevitable uncertainty that life throws at you.

10

Thriving in Uncertainty

"The journey of a thousand miles begins with one step."
  Lao Tzu

Momentum isn't only built when life feels predictable; it's built in the moments where the next step is uncertain. Uncertainty triggers the part of the mind that craves safety and familiarity. When the path ahead isn't fully visible, old beliefs, doubts and 'stay where you are' narratives tend to surface. But uncertainty isn't the enemy – it's information. It shows you where you default to comfort and where your internal filters need updating. Thriving in uncertainty means recognising these patterns and choosing to move with clarity rather than fear.

"I don't know HOW to get there."

One of the biggest stumbling blocks is how to achieve your goals. You know where you are and you know where you want to get to, but how do you get there?

Imagine for a moment, the desired outcome is to bake and eat your very own cake (Who doesn't want to have their cake and eat it?) and then seeing perfectly made cakes everywhere, but having no idea how the cakes are made. If you've never baked a cake before and you don't have a recipe, where do you start? The logistics of getting from A to B, working out what ingredients were needed, the quantities, the order you put them in, where you get them from in the first place, the temperature of the oven and how long to bake the cake for.

It becomes even more confusing when different people tell you there are different ways to bake the same cake. Approaching cake baking with all of these unanswered questions can feel overwhelming, usually leading to mental paralysis and not taking any action. Without action, there will be no cake... or anything else for that matter!

When you look at getting from A to B that way, it definitely puts you at a disadvantage, because the truth is, you won't know how to bake a cake if you haven't done it before. If everyone knew how to do everything before they ever did it, then there would be nothing new to learn.

Dreaming with the Brakes On

When it comes to creating your dream life, you really shouldn't know how you're going to achieve it and if you do, then the chances are it isn't as big a goal as it could be. Goal setting is usually carried out within the limitations of a person's thinking. This includes the beliefs they have about themselves and what they are capable of and it's the reason that setting small goals is so common – it keeps people feeling safe. One of the biggest fears is the fear of failure and when you dream big, there is a higher probability that failure is possible.

Better to play it safe and achieve what you know is probable than to dream big and risk not getting there, right?

No!!!

Lowering the bar so you can tick the "win" box might give you a momentary boost, but it rarely leads to lasting motivation. In fact, it's one of the fastest ways to lose it. When your goals are too easy - things you already know how to do and just need to execute – they just keep you busy, but not fulfilled.

Doing something new might mean asking for help, developing new skills, stepping outside your comfort zone, or working with a coach to shift your mindset and overcome procrastination. That's the real work; it's where the transformation happens.

When I say "dream big", I'm talking about the goals you

quietly think about when no one's watching. The ones that feel just out of reach, the ones you may not even say out loud because part of you wonders if they're *too* big, *too* bold, or *too* unrealistic. That's how you know you're dreaming big.

Yes, big dreams will feel far away. That's okay. That's actually the point and that's also why milestones matter. They help you track progress, take in feedback, adjust your approach and most importantly, keep moving. When the distance between where you are now and where you want to be feels too big, overwhelming, it's easy to put things off. *"One more day won't matter..."*, but milestones change that. Having markers will not only hold you accountable, but it will also break down what can appear like an impossible mission into smaller, achievable goals. They give your unconscious mind something tangible to work with, something to aim for now, not someday.

And when you hit those milestones, celebrate them rather than just rushing on to the next. You might think you'll be content when you "finally get there," but the truth is, your unconscious mind is wired to continually seek more. It's one of its primary roles, which is why we are able to continually evolve. Without motion, things stagnate. Take time to acknowledge your progress – train your brain to associate pleasure with progress.

One more thing: your big dream doesn't have to match anyone else's. You don't need to want a private jet, a beach villa, or a personal chef... unless that's genuinely part of *your* vision. Maybe your dream is to have freedom in your schedule, or to live in a quiet home surrounded by nature. Maybe it's to compete at a high level in your sport or create a thriving business. Whatever it is, be honest about what you really want. Chasing someone else's dreams isn't true success.

Think about what the commitment is for you to actualise the dream. Do you really want it, or do you just like the thought of it?

Whilst being a professional athlete may sound appealing, are you ready and willing to do the training and follow the diet needed? Are you prepared to give up social events, wake up early, deal with injuries, not see your family and have the majority of your time totally focused on your sport?

The resistance to what comes with the goal will eventually play out and prevent you from achieving it. If the reality of having the dream isn't what you really want, it's better to be honest with yourself now, rather than find out later. Use the energy you have to create what YOU truly want for yourself.

Taking the First Step

It all begins with the end in mind – your goal, the destination you've keyed into your mental Sat Nav so you know the direction you're heading. You also know there are going to a number of steps involved to get there. How many... who knows? The great thing is, your only job right now, in this very moment, is to take the first step. That first step will start the process of moving yourself towards it

Before you even take the first step, your mind may kick and you find yourself thinking, *But what about all the steps in-between?*

It doesn't matter!

"It's not knowing what to do, it's doing what you know."
  Tony Robbins

If your goal is to bake a cake and eat it, but you don't know how to get from start to finish, the first step could be to find a recipe. Only when you have found your recipe will you take the next step, which could be finding out where to buy the ingredients from to give you the cake you want. You could end up going straight to a supermarket, but oops, it sells Chinese food rather than the sugar and icing you were looking for. Have you failed? Should you give up?

Remember, there is no failure, only feedback. You learn from the experience and next time you look at where to go before just turning up. Once you have sourced and purchased your ingredients, you're on to the next step. One step at a time.

Taking the first step is crucial for so many reasons. One being that you are showing the universe and your unconscious mind that you mean business. Saying you want something and then going on with life as usual isn't going to change anything. The goal sets the aim and activates your RAS. Your RAS is now on high alert to look for information that is important and relates to your goal. When you take the first step, your unconscious mind becomes even more focused – the message you send is that it's happening, you're doing it, you're making progress, you're taking a step, even if it's only a small step, it's still a step. Your RAS will begin searching for the next steps for you!

If you're hoping someone will tell you what to do so you can go and do it, what you're really looking for is certainty in how it will happen. Certainty is often the avoidance of uncertainty and the unknown is viewed as a scary place for most people.

"You don't know what you're walking into."

"Better to be safe than sorry."

"Better the devil you know."

"At least you know what you're getting into."

Common phrases to feel better about not stepping outside of what's comfortable.

If I had carried on using that mindset, I would still be in a toxic relationship. I would've continued to think, *Yes, he was cheating; yes, he treated me badly, but at least I knew what I was getting, so there were no surprises.* It felt terrible being there, but I'd gotten used to feeling bad; it actually felt comfortable because I didn't have to think about it and so it was easier to navigate.

These beliefs are used as the reason to 'settle' in life and avoid making mistakes and suffering because of it. Settling doesn't work because you know you are destined for more; otherwise, you wouldn't be reading this book right now. Allow yourself to dream big, knowing that if you can conceive it, then it can be yours.

Activation Tool – Courage Activation

Take a moment to write down any phrases that you may have used yourself, either now or in the past, to justify staying comfortable.

Go through each item on the list and ask yourself the following:

· **What is the belief I have about this?**

For example,

Statement: *Better to be safe than sorry.*

Belief: *I'm worried I'll fail.*

Statement: *At least you know what you're getting.*

Belief: *I'm scared that I won't know what to do.*

Using the list of beliefs you have uncovered, go through each one and ask yourself the following questions:

- **What would happen if it weren't true?**
- **How many ways do I know that it's not true?**
- **When has it not been true?**

You'll begin noticing all the ways those beliefs aren't accurate, which makes it easier to release them.

You can also use the activation point 'Bridging the Gap' in Chapter 5 to create your own stepping-stones to a new belief.

ACTION TIME!!

What is the very first step you will take towards your end goal?

Remember, you don't need to and shouldn't know all the steps in advance. You just need to get the ball rolling, your RAS will reveal the next step as you move – one step at a time.

Go and do it now!

If you are able, take that first step right now. Do it immediately!

If it's not appropriate this very second, put a date and time in your diary for when you will do it, ideally within 48 hours. Commit to getting it done. Tell someone you love that you're doing it and ask them to check in with you to make sure you have.

Once you've done it, congratulate yourself. Give yourself recognition – you've started! Celebrating the small wins will begin to create a positive association with taking action. All you need to do after that is decide what the next step is.

One step at a time leads to meaningful results!

11

Performing in the Storm

When you choose your thoughts, you choose your path.

It's easy to stay grounded when everything is going well and there's nothing out of the ordinary to deal with. But what about when it doesn't? That's the moment things get real and it's time to look at what staying on track actually looks like in practice.

One thing you can guarantee in life is that there will be a time when you will face some sort of adversity and whilst everyone's experience will vary in how hard those times may be, they will happen at some point. These hurdles are metaphorical forks in the road and you have the choice to go either way.

You can use them as the reason to give up or see them as an opportunity to recommit, double down and keep going!

I'm going through my own testing time as I write this very

chapter. In fact, it's the reason I chose to include it and I also believe that may very well be the reason I'm experiencing it. I'm sure that giving a real-life account of how to put this stuff into action when life gets a little bumpy will be of immense value.

Every tragedy, every setback, every hardship we face doesn't have to be about just getting through it. It can also be used as a chance to evolve and come out the other side thriving.

In Chapter 2, we touched on the universal laws, one of which is the Law of Rhythm. All things rise and fall. For every up, there is a down; for every high, there is an equal low. The pendulum must swing in both directions in equal measure. When times are really tough, there has to be an equal positive that follows.

It's only fair that I share with you what I'm going through and how I use these practices every day to stay positive, focused and come out the other end stronger.

I recently found a lump in my breast and the following day, I was told I was being referred as a high-priority case to check if the lump is cancerous. Right now, I'm in a state of limbo.

I'm not going to pretend that understanding how the mind works means I never feel emotional. All emotions have their place – we're here to experience the full spectrum of what it means to be human. Negative emotions are part of that and they have so much value, acting as feedback that something isn't in alignment with our values. When the things that are important to us are being violated or not being met, emotions

221

will present themselves to let us know. The question is, are you listening? Pushing them down and pretending they don't exist doesn't make them go away; it makes them stronger - what you resist persists – this is true of emotions. Listen to the feedback they are giving you.

When the doctor said I needed to see somebody soon, if I'm honest, I initially didn't feel anything. I went into survival mode and I just thought about all the practicalities. My diary was packed for the next few weeks, so I'd have to speak with my business partner about having a day off to go to the hospital. I had a training call that evening, so my focus was completely diverted back to that. It wasn't until later on, after the call had finished, that I began to even think about what had been said in the doctor's surgery.

I didn't sleep well that night, but I didn't think much either. I was just awake and my mind was blank. It was only when I got up the next morning that I began to feel emotional and I needed to cry. I let myself! Crying is a release of energy, which is why it can feel so good after a big old sob. When you feel like crying, do it. Holding tears back is like squeezing into a pair of trousers with a waistband that is too tight. When you loosen the waistband, you can breathe properly again and it's the same with tears; you will feel better. Maybe a little tired at first, but better for letting it out.

Next, I decided to write down my thoughts and feelings. Up until that point, I hadn't really had many, or I hadn't consciously acknowledged them, but once I started writing, they came flooding out. A great way to process what is going on internally is to write without thinking. Allow your unconscious mind to take over and say whatever needs to be said – writing for yourself only, knowing that no one else will read it. When you write something thinking that someone else will see it, it influences the words you choose by how much you are willing to share and the opinion you think they may have, so do it just for you. If you're angry, write it down. If you're sad, write that. Getting it out of your head and onto paper helps to stop thoughts bouncing around non-stop. It's like a shopping list – until you have written it down, you hold the items you need in the back of your mind. When you put pen to paper, you can forget about them until you go shopping.

I'm not comparing a shopping list to the traumas that people experience in any way. What I do want to demonstrate is that aside from the emotions that go with it, the unconscious mind doesn't know the difference between a shopping list and thinking about how someone will survive financially or get through an illness when it comes to processing information. Either way, if it's out of your mind and on paper, some of that processing can stop, even if just for a short while.

After spending about 30 minutes writing down everything on my mind, including thoughts I wasn't aware of, I felt lighter. I had mentally emptied out and felt able to take a minute. It was only then that I reflected on what was going on and what came to mind may well sound bizarre to most.

I love understanding human behaviour, so I couldn't help but consider how interesting the last 24 hours had been. 'Interesting' may sound like a bit of an odd word given the

223

situation, so let me elaborate.

Monday afternoon, the day of the lump finding.

On Monday morning, the lump didn't exist in my reality and so I had no feelings about it.

Monday evening, the finding of the lump.

The lump now exists and I plan to get it checked to make sure I'm okay. No need for concern.

Tuesday afternoon, the examination.

The doctor feels the lump and also finds some hard tissue surrounding the outer area and lumps under the armpits. I'm referred to as an urgent case to check if there is any cause for concern. I felt a little concerned.

In the 48 hours, nothing has actually physically changed in my world, yet my perception has. Although short-lived, I did play through the 'what if' scenario and of course, this is a possibility. The interesting part of this is that at the moment, whilst I'm writing this and I'm waiting for my appointment, I neither have nor don't have breast cancer.

To give you some idea of what I mean by this, I'm going to bring in an experiment known as 'Schrödinger's cat', which was carried out in the imagination of a quantum physicist, Erwin Schrödinger. It didn't actually take place.

In this experiment, a cat was placed in a sealed box with a device that may or may not release radioactive poison within the next hour, which would, of course, kill the cat. The odds were 50:50.

There was a 50% chance the device would go off and kill the cat and a 50% chance it wouldn't and the cat would live.

There are multiple realities going on and the cat is a blur of probability because until you open the box, the cat is both alive and dead at the same time. It's only the observation of something that makes it real. It takes the waves of possibility and collapses them into a particle through observation. Of course, when you look in the box, you will know if the cat is dead or alive, but up to that point, the cat is both dead and alive at the same time because both waves of possibility exist.

Bringing that back to the lump, I now know something that I didn't know before, i.e. there is a lump which may or may not be cancerous. I also know there are things that I don't know, i.e., whether or not the lump is cancerous. At this very moment in time, I have multiple realities of possibility that exist, which means I also have a choice.

I could choose to focus on, observe and look at the one where I am diagnosed with cancer. That is one possibility. Another possibility is the one where I am told it is a cys,t and I can go home a little more lumpy than I used to be. Both possibilities exist at the same time until I am told either way. When I wake up in the morning, it will be just another Thursday, no different from the one just gone. The only thing that would make it something other than that is my thinking about it. Until I see the specialist, I won't know what the outcome is, but the one I choose to focus on is the reality I will experience until that day.

Just like the cat, until the box is opened, the cat is both dead and alive, but thinking about the cat being dead before you actually know will probably make your experience in that moment feel not so good.

The point of all of this is that, right now, I am living in a space of possibility in terms of knowing for sure what the lump is and I know the version of reality I choose to think about and focus on will be one of the most significant factors in how good or bad I feel today. I'm choosing to see myself and focus on having a glass of something fizzy to celebrate the doctor giving me the all-clear.

This isn't about putting my head in the sand and I know I may wobble at times; it's about working with the things that are within my control. I cannot control how quickly my appointment comes through. I cannot control the news the doctor gives me, but what I can control is where to purposefully place my attention between now and then. I can also make sure I look after myself physically to ensure I feel as good and positive as possible, making sure I get plenty of good, nutritious food, sleep, exercise, fresh air and water. The way you feel physically has a massive impact on the way you feel emotionally, so always look after both.

I genuinely believe there is always something to learn from

everything that happens in life and that learning can be used to make positive changes in the future, changes we may not otherwise have had the opportunity to know about.

My learning so far: I can choose how to navigate my way through this period of the unknown. My thoughts and where I place them are my responsibility. If I feel emotional at times, that's okay; I'm human. How long I decide to stay wallowing is up to me. I will only ever be given the things I am able to handle; therefore, I can get through anything that comes my way.

I have to be totally honest here and confess that lumps haven't been something I check for regularly, but it was something my mind told me to do.

Learning number two: when I get those hunches, those intuitions, trust myself! Intuition isn't mystical; it's your unconscious mind processing information faster than you can consciously explain. Your unconscious mind knows more than you may think, particularly when it comes to your body, so listen. Your unconscious mind knows the blueprint for perfect health, which is why it also knows when we have anything less than that. The number of times I have thought I should do something and then brushed it off, only to later find I was right.

Activation Tool – Taking Control

This particular activation is super useful when difficult times present themselves, which they inevitably will at some point.

- **Get everything out of your head and onto paper**

Write down what you are feeling, thinking and saying to yourself. Get it all out, even the things you think you shouldn't say or feel. Anything that comes to mind should be written down until you have completely emptied out.

During this process, let your emotions out too. If you want to cry, cry. If you want to scream, scream. Holding emotions in doesn't make them go away, but it can leave you feeling like a balloon that is about to burst. Let a bit of air out so there is room to expand into again if needed.

- **Be kind to yourself**

Like all of the work in this book, this is optional, but it's one thing I find very powerful. Do something nice for yourself that adds to your well-being, rather than taking away from it.

It can be easy to forget to look after ourselves when things get tough. I used to reach for the wine and takeaways during times of stress. I didn't feel like cooking and I wanted something to take the edge off and help me relax, but I only ever ended up feeling worse than before. Then I had the stressful situation to deal with, plus the lethargy that followed a period of indulging.

That could be as simple as taking a long, hot bubble bath, booking in for a massage, or taking some time out for a walk. The better you feel, the better the situation will feel! Everything is a reflection – the Law of Correspondence – as within, so without.

Controlling the Controllable

Let's talk about the 'what if' frame of mind. The 'what ifs' can lead you down a path that you probably won't thank yourself for. It's usually the road to feeling overwhelmed.

I almost found myself going there after I bumped into my hairdresser a few days after my visit to the doctor, whilst still waiting for my appointment to come through. The thought went through my head that if it were the worst-case scenario and I lost my hair, he wouldn't be cutting it for me anymore and I love my trips to get my mop chopped.

It was a fleeting thought and I caught myself very quickly so that I didn't spiral down a rabbit hole with no way out. I realised I was focusing on things that were outside of my control and what I didn't want to happen. When you do that, you will feel out of control.

This isn't limited to times of pressure or strain; this goes for life in general and spending time attempting to control things that are outside of one's control is something that many people do every day. There are discussions day in and day out about the news and what has been reported that day and there is often a lot of emotion that goes with it. The reality is that there is very little, or probably nothing at all, that you can do about the government, the economy, or other people, so trying to change those things is one way to feel out of control.

When I thought about my appointment, the results that will follow and how my parents would cope if I were sick, I felt completely overwhelmed about things I can do nothing about and may not even happen.

"I have spent most of my life worrying about things that never happened."
  Mark Twain

Worrying about things you can do nothing about changes nothing, except the way you feel, which is everything. Trying to change things you have no influence over creates a mindset of defeat and frustration and it can lead to generalising the experience across other areas too. If someone is feeling frustrated that the price of holidays abroad has increased by 50% that year and their energy is being used to complain about it, thinking about how wrong it is and focusing on what will happen because of it, this is totally disempowering. That frustration and the mentality that life is just happening and they can do nothing about it will most likely end up flooding into their life in many other ways too, from their workplace, their children's school, the price of grocery shopping, because we take ourselves with us wherever we go. The vibration we are emitting attracts more of it. Your RAS will look to bring you the things you focus on, whether they are wanted or not. That is when it really does become overwhelming!

There are some things in life that we may not completely be in control of, yet we can influence the direction they take. These are usually connected to the people we interact with closely and therefore have the potential to make changes along the way. That said, there are no guarantees, because we are not magicians capable of jumping into the minds of others and changing the decisions they make. This is again where a lot of people direct their focus when attempting to change circumstances – spending endless hours trying to get their teenager to behave differently, their boss to manage staff with more compassion, their partner to eat more vegetables. This can sometimes work, but if I were a betting person, I would say the odds are not going to be in their favour.

You may be wondering what you should focus on, because most things will always be outside of your control and that is the whole point. Most external things in your life you will have very little, if any, influence over, so my recommendation is that you don't even bother. Feeling annoyed because you can't change something you have no power to change is a vicious cycle with no exit and it uses a lot of energy that could be better spent elsewhere, working on the things you can control, the things that will actually make the biggest difference.

Imagine an athlete has been preparing for months for a major event. One week before the big day, they catch a virus that knocks them off their feet. They can't train - the timing couldn't be worse. It's infuriating, but unless they're in control of biology and event dates, it's out of their hands.

Person A gets stuck in frustration. They mentally check out, telling themselves all the hard work was for nothing. They stop eating well, skip rehab and push away their coach's support. The setback drags on longer than it needs to, not because of the illness, but because of the reaction to it.

Person B, meanwhile, gives themselves space to feel disappointed, but then quickly shifts focus. They use the downtime to review performance footage, reflect on what's working, or strengthen mental strategies for pressure moments. They listen to their body, speed up recovery and start prepping for the next opportunity: same setback, completely different trajectory.

Now, let's look at this in business.

A startup founder has been working on a product launch for six months. Just days before going live, a major competitor releases something almost identical, with more funding, a bigger audience and more influence. It would be easy to feel deflated. They can't control what the competitor does.

Founder A becomes paralysed. They compare, panic and start doubting everything. They delay the launch, spend weeks tweaking things and lose the momentum they'd built. Eventually, they put something out, but it falls flat, mostly because they lost their own energy in the process.

Founder B feels the same initial sting, but quickly shifts their attention back to the plan. They double down on messaging, get creative with their value proposition and focus on their customers. Maybe they even lean into the competition as proof there's market demand. Instead of shrinking, they adapt and build trust by staying consistent.

In both examples, the initial blow is the same. The difference lies in where attention goes next.

You can't always control the conditions. You can't control the market, the weather, your competitors, or a last-minute curveball, but you can control your focus, your effort, your attitude and your response and that's what determines your next outcome.

Letting go of what you cannot control gives you the capacity to get creative and feel empowered in any situation.

Take responsibility for what's yours. Let go of the rest.

During the 2020 Covid-19 lockdown, I was a new business owner and so didn't qualify for any business support or personal grants from the government. At that time, I was running classroom-based training and so became unable to deliver my service in the usual way. This was one of the biggest tests of resilience I have ever had in my life. Not only was the newly created business model not able to function in the way originally planned, but I also had no income to support me over the period of adjustment I had to make. There were an exaggerated number of circumstances that were outside of my control. My partner and I had also just moved into a new property the month before lockdown and our outgoings had increased by some margin. The business was on track to do very well that year, but one by one, people were cancelling their courses. They were concerned about their own finances and being unable to work and so didn't want to pay for training that didn't appear like it would be able to go ahead, at least not in the way they had originally signed up for. My life felt overwhelmingly out of control. Up to that point, I'd always had the mindset that the worst-case scenario when it came to the business was that I could go and get a job and move to a smaller, more affordable property, which I was okay with. Suddenly, jobs were few and far between and any opportunity to move house had been taken off the table. There were no viewings. The world had come to a standstill.

I had to take a deep dive inside myself to pull out internal resources I didn't know I had and may not have ever been aware of if lockdown hadn't happened in the way that it did. I had to go back to the drawing board of everything I knew and pull out every tool in my toolkit to stay resilient and focused. My starting point was carrying out the Activation Tool exercise below.

Activation Tool – Stability Builder Framework

This exercise will give you clarity about what you can control and where to put your focus. Keep it really simple.

- **Draw a circle on a page, then draw another around that circle and then draw another around that circle. In the outer circle, write 'Out of Control'. In the middle circle, write 'Influence'. In the inner circle, write 'Control' (see image 3).**

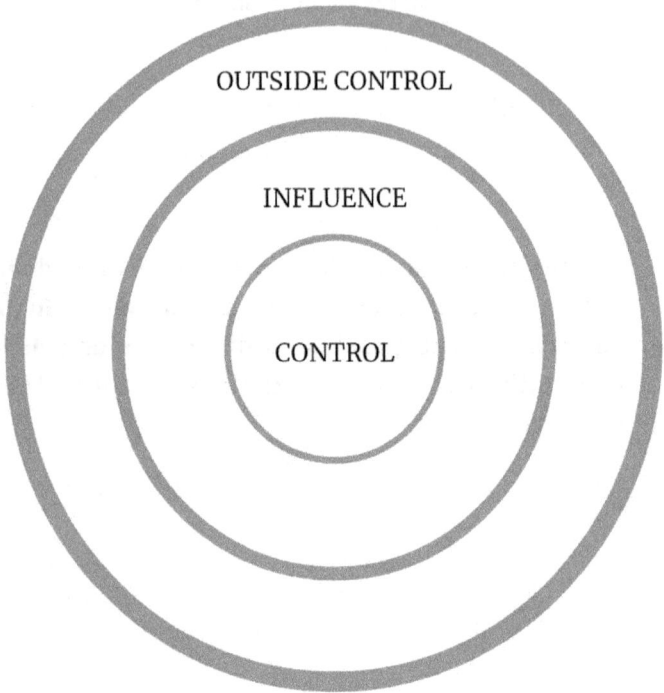

Image 3

Answer the following questions.

· **What is outside of my control?**

In the outer circle, make a list of everything that is outside of your control that you think about, feel any kind of emotion towards, or even try to control.

In the outer circle, list anything that affects your mindset or performance but is ultimately outside your control.

These are often the very things that keep people up at night and leave them feeling physically exhausted and powerless to make any positive shifts in their lives.

Examples include:

- Other people's opinions
- Market trends
- The behaviour of your competitors
- The government
- External feedback or reviews
- Company layoffs or restructures
- The weather
- The economy
- The traffic

Letting go of these frees up mental space. Acknowledge them, then release them. Energy spent here often gives zero return.

- **What is within my influence?**

In the middle circle, make a list of what you can't directly control but can influence.

You may have access to the people involved or be able to assist and direct change in this area, but it's not totally within your control.

Some examples include

- Your children,
- Team dynamics
- Project timelines
- Client or stakeholder buy-in (via how you present ideas or build trust)
- Your manager's perception of your work
- Collaboration from other departments

- **Finally, in the inner circle, list what is 100% within your control.**

These are your performance levers. Focus here delivers the greatest return on your energy.

Examples include:

- Your mindset and preparation
- Time management and planning
- Your physical health and recovery (sleep, nutrition, breaks)
- Asking for help or feedback
- Who you surround yourself with
- The quality of your work
- Your reactions under pressure
- How well you prepare for meetings, presentations, or tasks

- Your attitude and consistency
- Whether you learn from mistakes and apply feedback

This is your power zone. Investing here boosts resilience, confidence and impact - even in uncertain environments.

Take finances, for example. You might be facing a reality where there simply isn't enough money to meet every obligation right now. The credit card bill is looming, the cost of living has crept up and your income hasn't adjusted to match it. This is a scenario many people face, especially those balancing ambition with real-world pressures.

Here's the opportunity to focus on what you can do and it's where the shift begins. Even if you can't change the numbers overnight, you can still act. You can pick up the phone or write an email to open a line of communication. You can speak to your bank, your lender, or even a trusted advisor and say, "This is where I'm at. Let's work out a plan." It might feel like a small action, but in moments of uncertainty, these small actions are everything.

Taking ownership of a difficult situation changes the narrative. It moves you from a passive participant to an active player in your own story. Suddenly, you're not stuck; you're in motion. You're not waiting for things to happen to you; you're making things happen. That shift, though subtle, is profoundly powerful. It gives you energy and also helps you sleep at night. More importantly, it builds confidence and trust in you.

In any high-stakes or high-pressure environment, there will always be elements outside your control. You can't dictate a client's reaction, a colleague's choices, or an unexpected change in business strategy. But you can control how well you prepare. You can choose how you show up, how you respond and whether you keep communicating, even when it's uncomfortable.

It isn't about having control over everything; let's be real, that's never going to happen, but you could exhaust yourself trying. It's about developing the discipline to look at any situation and isolate the pieces you can act on. It's about taking those micro-moves seriously, knowing that momentum is rarely created by grand gestures but by consistent, thoughtful action over time.

Ignorance is not bliss! Pretending something doesn't exist doesn't make it disappear. When you face the things you need to deal with, you can then look at how you can overcome them and make a plan, even if you're not sure what that plan is to begin with. Ask yourself, "What's the next right thing I can do?" Then do it, no matter how small it feels, that's how progress is made.

The circumstances are what they are and you may not be able to change them, but what you can change is how you choose to respond to them. The more control you have over your well-being, the more in control you will feel about everything.

I have carried out this exercise many times throughout the years and each time I have felt calmer and more able to deal with what is in front of me at that time.

Just before I close off this chapter, I can confirm that all was good and the lump was nothing more than a cyst. What a tremendous blessing in disguise it turned out to be.

12

Transforming Setbacks

"If you want to be happy, be."
Leo Tolstoy

One of the most spoken about practices when it comes to shifting your thinking is to practice gratitude daily.

Something I did regularly and whilst I understood the concept, my intention behind it was somewhat misguided.

When I first started my practice, I used to make a list of all the things I was grateful for each morning when I woke up and for a while, it felt really good. That was until I noticed I was just saying the same things over and over again... my warm bed, a good night's sleep, plenty of food in the cupboard, a supportive and loving family, hot water, clothes to dress myself... The list went on. I was, of course, grateful for these things, but I soon discovered I was practicing gratitude from a point of lack rather than abundance. Whilst on the surface, being grateful regardless of where it comes from may seem like it's not a deal breaker, the feeling behind gratitude really does change the whole practice itself. Remember, you get what you focus on, whether you want it or not, so that feeling of lack in my gratitude practice was only going to give me more lack. My practice had become more about settling for the things I had in life rather than really going for the things I wanted and it's something I've witnessed with others who use gratitude as a tool to enhance their life, but end up creating the opposite effect. A client of mine experienced this very thing, which came to light early on in our coaching sessions. Many years ago, my client, whom we'll call Sarah for confidentiality reasons, came to see me because she was feeling unfulfilled but couldn't understand why. On paper, her life looked great, but something felt missing.

During one of our sessions, she told me about her childhood best friend, Jane. They grew up together, spent countless hours talking about their dreams and believed anything was possible. Sarah loved animals. She greeted every dog she passed on her way to school and was over the moon when her parents finally agreed she could have a pet. That passion sparked an early dream: she wanted to become a vet and one day own an animal sanctuary.

During one of our sessions, Sarah told me about her friend Jane, who'd she'd grown up in a small town. They were best friends and when they were younger, they enjoyed spending their time talking about the dreams they had for their lives. Their aspirations were big and exciting and they believed anything was possible. Sarah was a massive animal lover who would stop to greet every dog she passed on her walk to school. She begged her parents to have a family pet, until one day they agreed she could have a hamster. If she proved she was responsible and looked after it, they would consider getting a cat. After six months of pouring her love into her hamster, whom she named Mr Dominic, she was surprised and delighted when she came home to find a tiny little kitten waiting for her. Jerry the cat, named after the cartoon show Tom and Jerry, was soon following her around the house and cuddling her at night. Sarah made sure she fed, fussed and played with Jerry, along with cleaning out his cat litter tray every day. It was the final day of school before the summer holidays when Sarah's parents picked her up from school to take her to celebrate a year well done. She assumed they were heading to their local TGI Fridays, which was Sarah's favourite restaurant, so she was confused when they pulled up at the local animal sanctuary. Her parents led her inside and took her through to a room to meet the latest member of their family, a dog.

Sarah burst into tears of joy. She ran to meet what would soon become her best friend and companion. She named him Ben. By this point, she had found a fondness for Ben & Jerry's ice cream and so decided Ben the dog and Jerry the cat would make a deliciously amazing team. Ben was a stray who had experienced a lot of trauma, leaving him frightened to begin with. However, it didn't take long for him to open his heart and fall in love with Sarah and her family, just as they did him. Seeing the journey Ben had been through, from being rejected to being accepted and how it had transformed him from a sad and lonely dog to being happy, fun and content, lit a fire within Sarah. She knew she wanted to become a vet and own an animal sanctuary to help animals without a home.

Jane had witnessed the passion Sarah had for animals right from the day her hamster, Mr Dominic, arrived and she enjoyed every second of watching her play with and care for him. There were so many wonderful moments and Jane felt an urge to capture them so the friends would be able to look back at them and remember those times in the future. That Christmas, she asked her parents for a camera so she could do just that. Jane's love of photography grew and before long, her portfolio became a masterpiece of work that, in Sarah's opinion, would challenge even the greatest of all time. Jane had big goals to become a travel photographer, travelling the world and capturing its wonders through her images.

Both girls were so passionate about their goals and ambitions and they were equally excited about each other's dreams and what they could achieve.

Both attended sixth form to gain their A levels. Sarah took a year out to earn some money before heading to university, whilst Jane decided to bite the bullet and took a job abroad as a photographer's assistant. She saw this as the first step to pursuing her dreams. The following 12 months flew by. Jane demonstrated amazing ability in her role and ended up with a few of her very own clients. Meanwhile, Sarah had found herself a job where she happened to meet a really nice guy and fell head over heels in love. Her plans to go to university dwindled out. She didn't want to leave her new man right now; she was happy and her work paid reasonably well for her age, so life was good.

As the years went by, Jane and Sarah continued to keep in contact, either by email, phone, or the odd meet-up. As time passed, those occasions became less frequent and their connection was mainly through liking each other's posts on social media.

A few years had passed when Jane dropped Sarah a message to let her know she was in the area and would love to meet. She couldn't wait to hear all about Sarah's life and what had changed since they last got together.

When they saw each other, there were lots of hugs, kisses and tears. They felt so comfortable together, just like they always had all those years ago. Jane began by telling Sarah all about the places she'd been, the people she'd had the opportunity to work with and the plans she had coming up. She showed Sarah some of her amazing photography and she was positively beaming.

After a lot of nattering, Jane shifted the focus to Sarah, who immediately showed her the photos of the new addition to her family, a little cockapoo called Charlie. This prompted Jane to ask Sarah about her plans for university and her dreams to become a vet and have her own animal sanctuary. It was the first time in a while that Sarah had even thought about those plans. She explained to Jane that whilst that would be lovely, she had to be realistic. She had responsibilities and there were things she needed to take care of. Sarah had made the decision that she had to grow up and get her head out of the clouds because she had bills to pay. After her whirlwind romance, which eventually ended, she found a new partner. They'd decided to buy a house together and so she needed to stay in her job until she had saved up a deposit. The job had become very mundane very quickly, but she was doing it for a reason, so it was serving a purpose for her. At the time, she convinced herself it was only temporary and she would revisit the whole animal thing at a later date. Admittedly, it had gone on longer than planned, but it was still just a stepping-stone to get her set up, ready to take the leap. Once she had a mortgage, then it would be the right time and she could consider her options.

It was another few years before they caught up again and updated each other on what they had been doing since they last met. Jane was now living in New York and travelling all over the world with her photography. She'd met a guy along the way and married him in a small beach ceremony six months earlier. They were going to take an extended honcymoon the following year, travelling around Europe. The great thing with Jane's work was that she could do it from anywhere in the world and she loved it so much that she would do it even if it wasn't work.

Sarah then told Jane about her latest job, one she wasn't particularly enjoying, but the pay was a step-up from the previous and it came with a promotion. This was good, but it also meant she had more responsibility, so she was stressed a lot more often. All being said, it allowed her and her partner to go on holiday a couple of times a year and boy, did she need that! She now had the house she had been saving for, she was engaged, her wedding was fast approaching and in a couple of years, they would probably start trying for a family.

Jane loved hearing Sarah's news. It appeared she had created so many of the things she wanted, but she was curious if Sarah still dreamt of becoming a vet and having her own animal sanctuary. It was something she had been so passionate about and her plan had always been to revisit it at a later date. It came as a bit of a surprise to Jane when Sarah looked confused by her question. She had completely forgotten all about her dream and Jane mentioning it was the first time she'd thought of it for quite some time. It had faded into a distant memory, a childhood fantasy. She had become so ingrained in the day-to-day of life that she rarely gave any thought to her dreams anymore. Those things had been put on hold a long time ago so she could focus on what she thought she needed in her life at that time.

What Sarah said left Jane feeling saddened. It was a story she'd heard many times before from the many people she'd met along the way.

Sarah told her the big things in her life were taken care of, which, in her world, meant her mortgage, a pension plan and a husband-to-be – things most people would see as being big achievements, markers of doing well. She then added that she didn't need anything else, so she really should be grateful for what she has. She may not be a vet or have her own animal sanctuary, but others were way worse off. Whilst she wasn't happy or fulfilled in her job, it paid the bills, which was more than many people could say these days.

In the space of a few years, Sarah had gone from thinking about the extraordinary life that she wanted – having her own vet practice and animal sanctuary – to the life she felt was necessary: having a mortgage, a good job, a pension – to a life she was willing to settle for, a life where at least the bills were paid. She used the things she thought she should be happy about by most people's standards as her reason to feel grateful, because life could be worse. Her gratitude was based on a comparison of other people's situations. Sarah reasoned that she had many things to feel grateful for: she could eat, she had her health, friends, a partner, a warm bed, things that so many take for granted as being a given. This is very true as it's easy to lose sight of just how fortunate and truly wealthy a huge number of the population actually are today. Whilst you may not have the latest iPhone, just the very fact that we have the ability to make calls across the world at any time of day is just mind-blowing! We have the world at our feet and all the opportunities that come with it and that really is something to be grateful for. And feeling blessed for the gift of where you are doesn't mean you shouldn't want more for yourself.

Gratitude is a beautiful and powerful practice and it's not about living from a place of, 'Life could be worse; I should just be grateful.' It's about taking time to appreciate the life you have and all the good things in it. It goes back to where you place your focus. When you spend time appreciating those very things, it's not just thinking it or saying it; you have to feel it, otherwise it's just words. I'm sure you've experienced a time when someone is saying the right thing, but you just know they are not feeling it. It's the same with gratitude!

Life can be so busy and it can be easy to allow yourself to get pulled into the never-ending rat race and lose perspective on what matters. There is always something new to buy – the latest phone, car, pair of boots, gadgets, clothes – and as soon as you have them, a new, even better one comes out. Wanting better for yourself is a good thing; we all deserve the best and we're programmed to continually strive for more. It can become a problem, though, when there is no time spent appreciating what is already present in our lives. We take ourselves with us wherever we go, so no matter how many new phones or cars someone creates in their life in the future, if they don't appreciate the life they have right now, they won't enjoy the things that follow.

When you notice just how much you have available to you already and focus your attention on it, your RAS brings even more to your attention.

Stripping things right back is a great way to appreciate how much you really have, things that are so often seen as a given. Taking the time to think about all the things that just happen for you every single day without thought – the kinds of things many only realise the value of once they are compromised or gone, the amazing miracles that take place every minute of the day.

When your health is not 100%, you realise how blessed you are to feel well.

If someone hurts you, you understand how good it feels when you're in love.

Being surrounded by people who drag you down heightens your appreciation for being with those who lift you.

Experiencing something's opposite brings into awareness how fortunate you really are. Gratitude is learning to appreciate those things regardless, not just because they have been or could be taken away. Those positive things are always there and it's easy to become numb to their existence and forget how many wonderful things we have in our lives.

Like every emotion we feel, gratitude has a frequency to it and that frequency vibrates at a high rate. Focusing on what you appreciate in life requires focus and our conscious mind only has the capacity to focus on one thing at a time. This means that if you give your full attention to the things you feel grateful for, the other negative emotions will not be present in that moment. You cannot feel grateful and angry at the same time – the frequencies are too far apart from each other. If your focus is on one, the other does not exist in that moment. When someone is truly feeling the emotion of appreciation, the waves of their emotions, the vibrations and wave cycles are formed close together, which increases the speed at which your desired and positive manifestations come into physical form. Tipping the scales more in the direction of what is wanted, even if just slightly, will cause shifts to take place in favour of them.

A Test of Gratitude

Let's get real. Being grateful when things are good can be easy. The days when everything seems to go your way: you wake up on the right side of the bed, your hair falls into place, you miss the traffic, you open your email to a big order, someone pays for your coffee... Oh, how lovely life is! Why wouldn't you feel grateful?

The real test of gratitude and the true meaning of it is putting it into practice when things are not going as you hope for and these are also the times when it's most powerful. Being grateful for the things that on the surface cause the most pain has the power to shift the meaning you give to those experiences and change your whole perspective about them and life.

I personally went through a period during the 2020 lockdown, when things did not go as planned, along with many other people in the world. I used this time to really practice working on my focus. Don't get me wrong, I spent a good couple of days feeling really sorry for myself and I'm sure most people would've said I had every right to. I felt worthless, like I didn't matter and completely powerless. In those moments, I did not feel grateful for an awful lot. The bits of gratitude that I lightly practiced during the first few days were definitely coming from a place of lack. I remember thinking something along the lines of, *I'm grateful that I'm locked in and no one can see me because I feel like crap.* I allowed myself to live at effect, fully. I decided the situation I was in was causing me to feel bad and there was nothing I could do about it. I took no responsibility and so I couldn't do anything about it. This got boring very quickly! I was fed up with hearing myself moan, particularly knowing what I know. If I had continued down that road, it was only going to get worse.

After the initial sting of not having any support from the government, I looked at where I did have support, both within myself and the support I had from others. I knew that, as I was fit and healthy, I could support myself physically to carry out whatever tasks were needed. I had my partner supporting me; he made me laugh every day. My parents were willing to move heaven and earth to make me feel good. My brothers would check in regularly and point out all the good things I had going for me. I had a lot of support and decided to focus on that.

When you're experiencing a problem, it can feel like you have a metaphorical box on your head and it's easy to lose sight of everything else that is going on around you – you filter your reality through the lens of lack and your RAS shows you plenty. Even through the worst of times, there is always something, even if it's the smallest thing in that moment, that you can be grateful for.

Practicing gratitude during the hard times is the most testing but also the most powerful personal tool. And when you do, it has the potential to change every challenging situation you ever face.

This is where the Law of Polarity really comes into play. If you've gone through something incredibly painful, that means its opposite must also exist - because you can't know one without the contrast of the other. Without sadness, joy wouldn't have any meaning. Without failure, success wouldn't feel like a win. This doesn't invalidate the pain; it just reminds you that contrast gives experiences their meaning. The challenge is, when you resist the tough stuff, when you try to block it out or push it away, you're not just putting your attention on it (which only magnifies it), you're also unconsciously shrinking your capacity to feel its opposite. It's like saying to yourself, *"I can't handle the intensity,"* so you close the door on the full spectrum. And when you do that, it limits what's available emotionally, energetically and even in terms of opportunity.

Take performance, for example. An athlete who chokes under pressure on race day might want to forget it happened, bury the disappointment and just "move on." But if they stop and reflect, they might find something in that experience - maybe they learned what focus really means under pressure, or they uncovered a pattern they'd never seen before. Being willing to feel the failure and still find something useful in it increases one's emotional range. They expand their capacity and the next time they're in a high-stakes situation, they don't fear the moment; they trust themselves to handle it.

When those testing times come along and they will, in those very moments, look for what you can be grateful for about the event, the struggle, or the situation that is taking place. Find something to appreciate about the thing itself.

During lockdown, I quickly began to appreciate the kick start it gave our business to innovate and look at new and improved ways to work. This is something that probably wouldn't have happened for years, if at all, had it not been forced. Necessity is the mother of invention after all. I also appreciated that it reconnected me with nature. In the months before lockdown, I had been doing most of my workouts at the gym and getting less fresh air than I like to have. Taking a daily walk wouldn't have happened so often without it. With restaurants closed, I appreciated the new dishes that my partner started cooking. I'm not going to pretend I got involved in the actual cooking side of things, but I did enjoy eating them!

It was also the time that I had the inspiration to write this book, so without it, you wouldn't be here reading this today. That, I am truly grateful for!

The most challenging times are the ones that give us the opportunity to grow the most. It's more common to only realise the benefits of a seemingly bad experience after the event. By seeking out the positive and looking for a reason to be grateful for it whilst you're going through it, you are one step closer to being the powerful creator you were born to be.

Your Greatest Teacher

I hold it close to my heart that we have the opportunity to learn from everything we go through, everything we experience, both what we see as good and bad. There is always something positive we can take from it that will improve our lives in the future. When we choose to see experiences as a chance to learn and grow, we are then able to view our experiences in a different light, knowing they have served us in ways we may not even be aware of until a later date.

Finding a lump left me reflecting and one of the first things I wondered was what I could learn from it. I quickly admitted to myself that I spend way too little time doing things that I enjoy outside of my work. I'm what many would label as a workaholic. I just see it as being passionate and determined and I know that to achieve the things I want takes more than working 9am to 5pm. I love what I do and I sometimes allow it to be all-consuming. What I have learnt is that there is no rush. I know my goals will continually grow as I do and so enjoying the other parts of life along the way is essential. I also know that my work will only benefit as a result of my being more rounded and whole as a person.

Events where there is no meaning found in the experience of them are the ones that will continue to have negative emotions associated with them, which makes perfect sense. When there has been a really difficult time in your life and the experience appears meaningless, it can leave you questioning what the point of it, or even life, is. When you can use those experiences to create a better future, you can more easily accept that they were part of the journey leading you to a version of you that you would never have tapped into or even known about without them.

No matter where you are starting from, your current circumstances or what you are working through right now, there will be a positive lesson in there, even if it's one you have to go searching for.

When you ask the right questions, the questions you want the answers to, you activate your RAS to look for those answers. You direct the focus of your mind to give you the solutions you seek.

The important thing to remember is that knowledge is not power; it's the application of that knowledge that is powerful and it's the same when it comes to lessons. Understanding what you have learnt from a situation is only part of the story; it's about how you then use and implement the lesson to make positive changes. From the things you have learnt, decide what you will do differently and take action towards doing it. Lessons are there to teach us and until we actually learn from them, we'll repeatedly come up against the same experiences. It may appear in different forms, but the lesson itself will be the same.

For years, I kept having situations come along whereby a significant person in my life would make a suggestion or a decision about what we should be doing and even though I wasn't sure about it or didn't think it was the right thing to do, I went along with it anyway. Almost every time, when things didn't work out, I proved myself right. I knew it wouldn't work, but I did it anyway.

This included everything from whether to go on a second date with someone I had my doubts about, to taking a job that didn't feel right, to choosing which dress to wear on a night out. Each time I let other people's opinions determine the choices I made, even though they weren't what I thought was best, I would end up in the exact position I didn't want to be in.

I was completely oblivious to the fact that it kept happening until one day, when I found myself thinking, I've done it again!

That was when I took notice and recognised that this kind of thing had happened more than once, which is usually a sign that there is a pattern going on. Remember those patterns – your thoughts, feelings and behaviours - exist in your unconscious mind, so most of what you do day in and day out is outside of your awareness. Becoming consciously aware of a pattern is the first step to changing it.

I asked myself what it was that I was repeatedly doing that wasn't serving me. The answer came to me that I wasn't trusting myself. I argued with myself for a while, questioning whether or not I could or should trust myself. The irony! I kept coming back to the same conclusion: the times I hadn't trusted myself were the very times that things hadn't worked out.

The lesson was that I can and must trust myself.

There is a key component when it comes to really benefiting from the experiences you have and incorporating the lessons learnt and that is all to do with the direction of your focus that follows.

When we first learn something, it's often focused on the mistake that we don't want to make again. The issue with that is that the direction of focus is then on what is not wanted or what you won't do in the future. Your unconscious mind processes the instructions you give it, whether it is about what you want or not.

I knew I had to learn to trust myself, but if I'd have said, *"My lesson is that I shouldn't trust other people,"* all my unconscious mind would have registered is, *"Trust other people,"* and the lesson would never be learnt. It's vitally important that you take the lesson and make it a positive lesson for you and this is really simple to do.

When you know what you don't want or won't do, which is often related to other people, just spin it around and look for what you *will* do instead, something that will positively help you in the future.

For example, *"Rather than not trusting other people, I will trust myself."*

This will activate your RAS to focus on and bring into your awareness all the ways to do that very thing.

Activation Tool – Rapid Debrief

Time to learn from your experiences.

- **What positive lessons can I take from the unwanted experiences I am going through or have been through in the past?**

This is particularly relevant to events where there are still negative emotions present. Really consider how it will help you in ways that wouldn't be possible had you not had the experience.

If you keep thinking the same thoughts when events occur, ask yourself the following question:

- **What am I not paying attention to that I need to?**

Your unconscious mind will keep knocking on the door of your conscious mind until you answer. Listen!

What are the thoughts that keep coming up that get pushed to the side?

Maybe you keep telling yourself you need to take time out, but then you carry on regardless.

Could it be knowing you need to contact a certain person, but you keep putting it off?

Pick up a blank piece of paper and write whatever comes to mind. Listen and trust yourself.

Turning Knowledge into Power

The important part, then, is integrating the lessons. Remember, it's only when you put those lessons into action that your unconscious mind will stop giving them to you.

If you kept failing a driving exam with the same error each time, you wouldn't be given a driving licence. You also probably wouldn't just keep taking it over and over again, wondering why you're not passing. To be successful, you need to take the feedback on why you failed, learn from it and then apply those lessons. When you retake your driving exam using what you have learnt from your previous attempts, you are able to do it with new applied knowledge, which is power!

Activation Tool – Adaptive Integration

Taking your answers from the previous exercise, ask yourself the following questions:

- **How will I implement the lessons into my life?**
- **What positive changes will I make?**
- **What will I do differently knowing what I now know?**
- **How will this benefit me in the future?**

Make sure you focus on what you WILL do differently, rather than what you will avoid doing.

13

The Purpose-Performance Connection

Think like the person you are becoming.

You've made it to this point in the book and maybe you have put into practice all of the Activation Tools; maybe you haven't yet. Either way, that's okay. You have already come so far. This book is here for you to use as a working manual that you can come back to any time and use whichever Activation Tool you feel will serve you most. Wherever you are right now is perfect!

You have learnt so much about how your mind works, how you change your thinking, the basic mechanics of physical creation and the power of focus. You also had an insight into how to create a mindset for success, how motivation works, getting through failure and the tough times and using gratitude as a tool to learn powerful lessons that will ultimately make every experience, wanted or unwanted, one of benefit.

Now we're onto the magic of creation and I have to warn you

that what you are about to learn isn't rocket science! In fact, you have probably heard most of it a million times over already and you may even be bored with hearing it.

I've also said this several times throughout this book, but it's worth repeating as this isn't limited to this book; it's about everything you have learnt, may know already, or have read about in the past...

Knowing something doesn't change anything; you have to do something about it!

There are varying studies that show people have to digest information a number of times before it actually sinks in. This theory has been applied across advertising and marketing with what's known as the 'marketing rule of 7', developed by Dr Jeffrey Lant. The rule states that a potential customer must interact with a message at least seven times before they'll take action to buy it. Applying the same principle to your life, reading this right now could be the seventh time for you – the piece of the puzzle that makes it slot into place. With the advancements of technology and information overload, who knows what number has grown over the recent years? Regardless of the figure, you get the idea.

Whilst none of this is magic, if you apply it consistently, then it certainly can feel as if there is something magical taking place.

Let's get creating!

I'm going to break down each part of the creation process into really simple steps that you can easily follow to achieve anything you want in life, in any area of your life, too.

Activation Tool – Purpose Alignment

Step 1: Discover Your Why

Find out your purpose, your reason for being here and for pursuing the things you want in the first place... Sounds big, right?

Where do you start?

A misconception is often that your purpose has to be a really big one that would have an impact on the whole world. This way of thinking puts so much pressure on you that it can leave you unable to think of a purpose grand enough to deliver on those expectations. I remember when I first realised that each and every person's purpose is different and the size of it is irrelevant, I was able to breathe a massive sigh of relief.

Your purpose is quite simply the thing that lights you up when you think about or do it.

This could be anything from creating delicious food for people to writing music, collecting antiques, sewing, sports, writing and everything in between. These are the things that make you feel fulfilled and even if you had all the money in the world, you would spend your time doing them anyway. Your purpose in life doesn't need to be a big, one-off, massive, life-changing thing that impacts hugely on other people; it's whatever lights you up, which will be something different for the next person.

Your purpose can change and it will change as you do. Oh yes, your purpose is not a one-hit wonder that you must get right or you'll never live a fulfilled life. Your purpose when you are 20 will very likely be different from when you are 45 and have had more life experience, maybe some children and you're in a different phase of life. This is a good thing; it means we continually have the potential to evolve.

It also doesn't always have to be career-related. There are many ways your purpose can be fulfilled. Someone might feel most alive when they're pushing their limits and showing others what is possible. That sense of purpose might show up through sport, business, or even mastering a craft. For example, they could set goals to compete at a professional level, or they might channel that same drive into coaching others, building a brand around a performance mindset, or leading a team in a high-pressure environment. It could be as fulfilling to lead with impact from behind the scenes as it is to stand on the podium. The key is recognising that the deeper purpose of growth, mastery and contribution can express itself in more than one way.

I once worked with a client who had walked away from a high-flying corporate role because, in his words, "It looked successful, but it didn't feel like success." What lit him up was structure, strategy and helping people perform at their best, not managing endless politics and ticking boxes for someone else's version of achievement. He ended up taking a role at a local sports club, running operations and mentoring young athletes. On paper, it looked like a step down. But in practice, he was thriving. He got to spend his days making a real impact, doing the kind of work that energised him. He wasn't chasing external approval; he was choosing alignment. Whether or not that ever led to a bigger platform or wider recognition didn't matter; he was already living a life that felt deeply fulfilling. Once you know what your why is in life, the rest will follow more easily. When setting any goals, keep your purpose in mind, checking whether they support it or take away from it.

If you are unsure or you want further help in discovering your purpose, head to www.themindreconstructor.co.uk/book-res ources, where you'll find your free Discovering Your Purpose exercise.

· **Complete the Discovering Your Purpose exercise.** When you live life on purpose and with purpose, you have the drive to keep going when most would give up, because it's about something so much bigger than a goal.

Step 2: Know Your Outcome

What do you want?

It sounds so simple and it is, yet it's one of the most overlooked steps in achieving what you want. Without this, the roadmap to get you there will be unclear and hazy at best. The more specific you are with your intentions and goals, the easier they will be to achieve.

YOU ARE ACTIVATING YOUR RAS!

Having a crystal-clear vision of where you are going gives a firm direction to your unconscious mind. This activates your RAS, the gatekeeper, which then filters through the external information and brings into conscious awareness that which is relevant to your goals – the rest is deleted, distorted and generalised.

Your unconscious mind will show you the easiest pathway to achieving the very thing you want. If you only have a vague idea about what you want, you miss out on the opportunity of bringing the very things that will lead you to your destination into your conscious awareness.

Just like the Sat Nav, whilst inputting a general direction is better than no direction at all, it doesn't guarantee where you will end up; in fact, nothing does. That said, being as specific as you can be about what you want certainly increases your chances of arriving there or somewhere even better than you imagined.

Maybe the idea of becoming laser-focused on one specific outcome makes you feel a bit uneasy, like honing in on one thing might cause you to miss out on other opportunities that could be just as good. It can feel logical to keep your options open, just in case something better comes along. You might even worry that by being too focused, you'll overlook things happening around you that could've led somewhere great. Rest assured, this is not the case.

Having a laser-sharp focus on where your life is heading points the compass towards the direction you want to take it in. The purpose of this is to home in your attention and activate your RAS, bringing the external possibilities around you into your physical reality – something you can see, hear, feel, smell and taste. You collapse the waves of possibility into a wave of probability by observing reality in your mind. That doesn't mean you will arrive at your destination in exactly the way you imagine and the destination itself may turn out to be slightly different, too. The focus will lead you to your outcome and it's essential to have flexibility along the way - this goes back to letting go of success – it may show up differently than expected.

If your goal was to play for a specific team in a particular division and you end up signing with a different team in the same league, does that mean you missed the mark? Not at all. You still reached the level you were aiming for. Sometimes, the exact version of what you want shows up in a different wrapper - the kit you wear might be a different colour, the badge on your chest might not be the one you originally envisioned - but the essence of your goal has been met.

It's easy to get hung up on the details of what you want and then forget to notice you have created the very things you set out to do.

The purpose of focus isn't to block out anything that doesn't match your exact vision; it's to give your mind and your RAS clear instructions about where you're heading. Universal forces are working behind the scenes to support that direction, even when things don't unfold exactly as you imagined. Remember, you don't have access to the full, bird's-eye view of your life. As much as we'd love to see the whole map, we're often only working with a tiny part of the puzzle.

Let's say your dream is to play for a specific team in your league because everything about it looks ideal - the branding, the coaches, the stadium, the kit. What you can't see, though, is that behind the scenes, that team may not offer the development opportunities, culture, or future potential that would really serve you. So, you get signed by a different team in the same division. It's not what you pictured, but it ends up being everything you actually wanted. That's the power of aligned outcomes: they don't always come in the exact packaging you asked for, but they arrive in a way that serves you better than you could've planned.

Take the time to really get honest with yourself about what *you* want to achieve, not what looks impressive to others, or what you think you should aim for. It's easy to default to goals that feel safe or socially approved, but if they don't light you up, they're not going to sustain your motivation for long.

Step 4: You Will Be Tested – Be Prepared

Setting goals is wonderful and setting them is the easy part. Achieving them, on the other hand, is unlikely to be as straight-forward as you expect. Things will come up; obstacles will appear to get in the way; there will be detours you didn't even know existed before you started and it's at these times that your resilience will be tested.

Giving up can seem like the easy option, but is giving up on your dreams ever really easy? They don't just disappear... they linger in the background, quietly haunting you, reminding you of what could have been.

If you've already taken that first step, you've done the part that so many people procrastinate over and find every excuse to avoid. That's huge! You're already ahead of the majority. And while it might feel hard at times, starting something new only to hit the same blocks again doesn't make things any easier. It makes far more sense to keep going, work through the resistance and grow from it, rather than keep resetting the clock every time it gets uncomfortable.

Obstacles aren't here to stop you; they show up as an opportunity for you to demonstrate how committed you are to yourself and your goal. Every challenge is a chance to stretch, to step more fully into the version of you that's actually capable of holding the success you're aiming for.

"Challenges are what make life interesting and overcoming them

is what makes life meaningful."
 Joshua J. Marine

Seeing the walls, the hurdles, the obstacles and the detours as a chance to grow gives them a whole new meaning. They are given to you to build character- something you wouldn't have had without the experiences that present themselves when you push yourself.

At first glance, a metaphorical wall can appear quite daunting, especially if it's one you haven't encountered before. Or, that wall can be your biggest adventure if you choose to see it that way. When you ask yourself how you can get around it, climb over it, find people to give you a leg up, build a bridge, knock it down, or countless other ways, your RAS will show you how to do it. It's about asking yourself the questions you want the answers to!

Another powerful tool is mental rehearsal - and not just for visualising the wins. It's just as important to mentally walk yourself through the moments that don't go to plan. If you know there are likely bumps in the road, the kind that could throw you off track or make you question it all, then plan.

Think about how you'll respond when it gets hard (because at some point, it will), when motivation dips, or when things start to feel heavier than expected. If you've mentally rehearsed your response, you're far more likely to keep moving forward instead of defaulting to old patterns or giving up altogether. It's not just about seeing the best-case scenario;

it's about being ready for the bits that most people use as an excuse to quit.

Visualising your life turning out how you want it to is of massive importance in directing your focus and activating your RAS and it won't always be straightforward getting there. No amount of positive thinking is going to take away the challenges that will come up.

The saying 'what doesn't kill you makes you stronger' is true. When you're pushed to your limits, even if those limits are relatively small in comparison to other people's or even other areas of your own life, you have to grow to meet and overcome them. It's a mental and emotional workout that leaves you with more strength and flexibility when you get to the other side.

If the goal is to write a book by a specific date, then you will have to do some writing. The task of writing may well feel easy when you're inspired on a Tuesday morning after a good night's sleep, but what about a Friday evening, when you're feeling tired and not in the mood? What if your diary is packed with day-to-day obligations so the only writing time available is at, say, 5am on a Saturday?

If the goal is to lose weight, what will you do on a sunny Saturday when your friends are having a cold glass of prosecco and nibbles in the garden and you're meant to be heading to a spin class?

If you've set an intention to make more money, then it's wise to ask yourself: how will you handle it when an unexpected bill lands, or you don't have the funds to buy something you really want that month? How will you stay focused when life throws a curveball... because it will. That's not being negative, it's being prepared.

Temptation to give in or give up tends to show up early, often not long after you've committed to something new. It's your unconscious mind throwing a challenge your way to check how serious you are. A test. Are you in or not?

It's a bit like what sometimes happens in relationships (I'm not saying this is healthy, it's just a helpful analogy). One person might test the other to see how committed they really are. They'll push, withdraw, or offer an easy exit and they want to see whether the other person stays or runs for the hills. If they stay, that signals that they're fully in.

The same can happen internally. The moment you commit to a new relationship, for example, it's uncanny how suddenly you become more attractive to others. New people show up, opportunities pop in. Partly because your energy has shifted and partly because it's a check... how committed are you, really?

The universe works the same way with your goals.

You set your intention, take a bold step in a new direction... and then, without fail, the test arrives. It often shows up in the form of other appealing opportunities - or the exact thing you were ready to let go of, suddenly becoming more available, more tempting, or seemingly more aligned than ever before.

This happens a lot in performance settings. Say you finally commit to pursuing a higher level in your sport or going all-in on your business and just as you do, an opportunity pops up to return to something easier or more familiar - maybe even something that used to work for you. It might feel safer, more predictable, perhaps even fun. But deep down, you know it's not what you really want anymore.

I experienced this firsthand after committing fully to a new business - goals set, vision clear, I was all in. Within weeks, I was inundated with offers from the old world I'd stepped out of. Acting and modelling jobs landed in my inbox like clockwork.

It was a hard test. The work was familiar to me and, although it didn't satisfy or fulfil me, it was fun and it paid well. For a while, I questioned whether this was a sign that I should stay in that career. But then I remembered... this is the test. It wasn't a signal to retreat; it was an invitation to double down, reinforce the commitment I'd made and show I was serious about the direction I'd chosen.

It happens all the time. You take a few steps toward something new, a different career, a fresh business direction and suddenly the thing you are walking away from starts gaining momentum. That's when the doubt creeps in and you find yourself wondering if it's a sign to stay put.

Here's the thing: it's rarely black and white, but growth requires space. To let something new in, you have to let go of what no longer fits. If your energy is split, your unconscious mind will be getting mixed messages and won't know what to prioritise.

When your energy is split, your RAS can't prioritise the new direction, so opportunities slip past unnoticed, because, in that moment, your focus is on continuing with the old thing. The test isn't there to stop you, it's there to see if you're ready.

When the test shows up, use it as a powerful gift - because that's exactly what it is. It will give you so much clarity. If the goal you've been working towards isn't truly what you want, this is the moment you'll feel it. Just like in a relationship, when things are tested and someone secretly wants out, they'll see that challenge as their exit door and jump at it.

Before making any decisions, check if you're using the test as an opportunity to opt out because you really don't want it, or if it's because there are limiting beliefs about whether or not you can achieve it. Any limiting beliefs, negative emotions, conflicts, or things that need to change that are giving you an excuse to give up, rather than dealing with them. Those old patterns emerge to keep you in the comfort zone, where it feels safe. The moment you're tested is also an incredible opportunity to build your mental strength. When you feel the pull to give up but choose to stay focused and committed, you train your mind to back you up. You prove to yourself that you're not going to be easily swayed by old stories or shiny distractions.

When you pass the test and come out the other side, the

momentum you've created starts to build. That deep sense of alignment clicks into place, your RAS sharpens and your focus becomes even more laser-locked. Your unconscious mind – and the universe – registers your commitment and responds accordingly.

It's like pushing through a tough training block or staying focused during a dip in performance. The moment you want to quit but continue anyway - when you show up regardless of how it feels - you're strengthening not just your physical ability, but your mental edge. That's where identity is built and when things start to shift. The opportunities, the breakthroughs, the results - they begin to reflect the level of commitment you've shown - as within, so without – the Law of Correspondence.

Keep in mind that your unconscious mind will always look for the easiest route to achieving everything, which again is where your RAS comes in – it seeks to find the path of least resistance.

Preparing in advance for these events, the tests, the obstacles, the times that can feel like a struggle, means that even when they do show up, you'll have practiced them in your mind, seen yourself coming out the other end and you'll feel ready to deal with them.

Activation Tool – High-Stakes Readiness

When starting this process, it can really help to draw on past moments where you've felt challenged in your performance - or even ones you haven't experienced yet, but could see happening in the future.

· **Make a list of any potential obstacles that could come up.**

Write whatever comes to mind.

For example, *when I'm approaching a big event or competition and I'm not seeing the progress I expected, I tend to go into panic mode. I start questioning whether I'm good enough, whether I've done enough and I forget everything I know about staying focused and trusting the process. All that mental clarity I've been working on goes out the window and I find myself slipping into comparison, self-doubt, or even pulling back effort.*

· **Go through your list and imagine that scenario happening and notice how you feel.**

Ask yourself: Do I feel equipped to handle this?

If yes - amazing, you've got that covered.

If not, move into the following mental rehearsal:

Close your eyes and picture the situation playing out. Imagine watching it from the outside and seeing that it's a chance for growth.

Now imagine it going well. Despite the challenge, you handle it with confidence, you find solutions and come out stronger.

Then shift perspective and step into the scene, seeing it through your own eyes, so it's as if you're living it now.

Feel what it is to be that version of you - capable, focused and solution-oriented.

Remind yourself: *There is always a way when you choose to look for it.*

You know how your RAS works and you trust it to lead the way.

See the world through your new eyes; hear the sounds around you, the words you say to yourself, the feelings and notice the knowledge you have.

Then, allow that positive feeling to double in intensity and sit with that new, positive, powerful feeling for a moment.

Take a deep breath in...

Now, check in with yourself and notice how those old hurdles feel different.

Imagine a time in the future when they could come up.

Whereas in the past you wouldn't have known how to get around them, now you know you can.

You are able to step around them and keep moving forward with the knowledge you have gained because of them. Something that will only ever serve you well in the future.

"Do not pray for an easy life, pray for the strength to endure a difficult one."
   Bruce Lee

14

Practice Makes Perfect

Knowledge is of no value unless you put it into practice.

You've strengthened your mindset, built momentum, rewired old patterns and aligned your goals with who you want to become. But awareness and alignment are only the beginning. Real change comes from what you practice. You already understand enough about how your mind works to make meaningful progress from here - not by learning more, but by applying what you know.

It's all too easy to use learning and information-gathering as the reason to delay taking action, but one thing I can guarantee is that no amount of knowledge will ever change your reality. You have to put what you know into practice – to embody it

I could tell you all day long about how to ride a bike, but the quickest way to learn to ride is to do it. You may have stabilisers to begin with. You will probably fall off a few times, maybe even hurt yourself, but falling off is never the issue; the issue is staying off when you fall. Every time you climb back on that bike, you will have learnt something new – usually what doesn't work and how not to do it – yet without that experience, you wouldn't have known. And it's the same with life.

I worked with a client who was deeply passionate about improving their performance - they'd read all the books on mindset, watched endless videos of top performers and could talk fluently about high-performance habits and routines. They had all the theory, but they were stuck in the same place, feeling frustrated and wondering why nothing was shifting.

The truth was, they hadn't taken consistent action. They'd convinced themselves that they needed to know more before they could do more. They were waiting for the perfect moment – more time, more confidence, more certainty, but of course, that moment never came.

What they couldn't see was that consuming information had become a clever form of procrastination. It felt productive, but it wasn't moving the needle. Their RAS was tuned into finding reasons to delay and so it did exactly that, showing them why now wasn't the right time to act.

The best way to get ready is to get started, because the truth is that it's the only way. No one is ever ready to ride their bike without stabilisers and if you were to try and think of all the possible outcomes, all the things that could go wrong when you finally kiss those two little pieces of metal goodbye, you'd be frozen with fear.

The first time I took my stabilisers off, I pushed away from the kerb and began pedalling, slowly at first and then more quickly and I soon realised that going that little bit faster gave me momentum. When going slowly, I struggled to balance and I found myself overthinking every move I made. As soon as I allowed myself to trust that I would work it out and gained just a little more speed, the forward motion seemed to keep me upright and I was able to ride easily.

Much like riding a bike, the more you hesitate, the worse it feels and the harder it is. Holding back won't serve you. It's like slowly lowering yourself into a freezing cold swimming pool one limb at a time – oh so painful! Holding onto the warm air outside of the cold water only makes you long to stay comfortable, even if what you really want is to have fun in the pool. Whereas when you dive straight in, it's uncomfortable at first, maybe even a little painful for a second, but you soon get used to it. Letting yourself just go with it, fully immersing yourself and trusting that you'll be okay, allows it to happen.

You won't ever know if something is going to work beforehand and, in reality, if everything in life were guaranteed, it wouldn't be half as much fun. Imperfect action beats perfect knowledge every time. The challenge and achievement are what make it worthwhile, even if it doesn't feel that way at times. The energy of being half in and half out has a mixed frequency to it because you are literally sending out mixed messages.

"I want it…"

"I don't…"

"But I do…"

"I'm not so sure…"

This will lead to things coming and going - you start getting somewhere and then it slows down. This kind of energy is palpable in relationships. When a person seems fully in one minute, then pulls back the next, it leaves the other person involved feeling confused and unsure about how serious they are and so they don't know how to respond. Your unconscious learns through repetition. Every time you practice, you reinforce the identity you're stepping into. Commit to yourself fully – you deserve it!

Activation Tool - Clear Message

Think of the universe as your lover! The message you put out there is quite literally the vibration you are sending into the universe - send your unconscious mind a signal it cannot misinterpret.

- **How clear are you about what you say you want? Are the messages you give to your unconscious mind and**

therefore the universe, consistent or changing?

Notice if there are times when you think, feel, or act in a way that is opposite to what you want.

If so, continue with the following question:

· **If I did achieve the things I really want, what would happen? What will change that I feel uncomfortable about?**

Any uncertainty is an indication to the unconscious mind that there could be a threat. The unknown feels scary and the mind's number one job is to protect you, even if the results it produces aren't what you want.

Acknowledging that things will change and considering how that will impact you in all areas of your life is important. Not paying attention to the things you fear, or unconsciously pushing against them, can leave you in an endless loop or conflict of wanting something but fearing it at the same time. This exudes an incongruence in your energy, leading to variable results.

· **If that change happened, how would I deal with it? What could I do to make it work?**

Acknowledging that any doubts, fears, or conflicts all have a positive intention at their root will help you to see them in a new light, so you can be kind to your unconscious mind for doing its job. Beating yourself up and criticising yourself only hinders your progress. Your unconscious mind is like a five-year-old child, so treat it in the same way - with compassion and love. The more love you give, the more you get back and the better you will feel in the process.

15

A Message from Me

A place that holds your hand and guides you through each day
A world with every answer, showing you the way
A feeling you've come home, yet you'd never really gone
Because you are it and it is you, everything is one.

You've reached the end of this book, but not the end of your journey... not even close. I hope you're leaving with a clearer understanding of yourself. Everything you've read has been designed to help you recognise what was already there: your potential, your patterns, your power and your ability to create change.

If there's one thing I want you to take with you, it's this: you don't need to have every step figured out, you just need to begin. Your mind will meet you where you are and support you along the way.

There will still be days when you slip into old habits... that's normal. Nothing you've learned disappears just because you have a difficult moment. You simply come back to the tools, the awareness and the understanding you now have. That's what growth looks like.

You're capable of far more than you've given yourself credit for. You've done the work by reading, reflecting and challenging yourself. The next stage is simply applying it.

Thank you for trusting me to guide you through this. I hope this book becomes something you return to whenever you need grounding, clarity or a reminder of what you already know to be true.

Your RAS is ready and waiting to serve you; let it be your best friend.

Finally and most importantly, I mean this with all my heart, thank you for taking the time, your precious time, to read this book. I truly hope you have found some valuable insights and it will be a stepping-stone towards creating your world, from the inside out!

Bibliography and Recommended Reading

Allori, Valia, 'Quantum Mechanics and Paradigm Shifts', *Topoi*, 32/2 (2015), 313–323

Bandler, Richard and Grinder, John, *Frogs Into Princes, Neuro Linguistic Programming* (Moab, UT, 1979)

Bandler, Richard, *Using Your Brain for a Change* (Moab, UT, 1985)

Braden, Gregg, *The Divine Matrix: Bridging Time, Space, Miracles and Belief* (1st edition, Carlsbad, CA, 2006)

Dispenza, Joe, *Becoming Supernatural: How Common People Are Doing the Uncommon* (Carlsbad, California, 2017)

Dispenza, Joe, *Evolve Your Brain: The Science of Changing Your Mind* (Deerfield Beach, FL, 2007)

James, Tad and Woodsmall, Wyatt, *Time Line Therapy and the Basis of Personality* (2nd edition, Carmarthen, 2017)

Krasner, A. M., The Wizard Within: *The Krasner Method of*

Clinical Hypnotherapy, (Santa Ana, CA, 2001)

Three Initiates, *The Kybalion: A Study of the Hermetic Philosophy of Ancient Egypt and Greece* (Chicago, IL, 1908)

Gribbin, John, *In Search of Schrodinger's Cat* (1st edition, London, 1985)

Sage, Peter, 'The Art of Living in Through Me', YouTube, uploaded by The Real Peter Sage, July 2016,www.youtube.com/watch?v=fJ4PB6YVjxY

Stark, G., 'Light,' *Encyclopaedia Britannica*, 1 December 2021, www.britannica.com/science/light

Resources

Head to the website below to access resources, including the 'My Purpose Exercise' and 'Activation Tool Exercises', found throughout the book:

www.themindreconstructor.co.uk/book-resources

If you would like to find out how you can work with me further, head to my website:

www.themindreconstructor.co.uk

About the Author

Sian is an Internationally Certified Trainer of Neuro Linguistic Programming (NLP), Time Line Therapy®, Hypnotherapy, Master Coach and Breathwork facilitator. She has worked with hundreds of individuals, through one-to-one coaching and training programmes where she has accredited coaches worldwide, teaching them the skills to change their mindsets, improve their lives and help others to do the same.

You can connect with me on:

🌐 https://themindreconstructor.co.uk